What's Gone Wrong in America's Classrooms

The Hoover Institution
gratefully acknowledges generous support from

TAD TAUBE
TAUBE FAMILY FOUNDATION
KORET FOUNDATION

Founders of the Program on
American Institutions and Economic Performance

and Cornerstone gifts from

JOANNE AND JOHAN BLOKKER
SARAH SCAIFE FOUNDATION

Edited by Williamson M. Evers

What's Gone Wrong in America's Classrooms

Hoover Institution Press   Stanford University   Stanford, California www.hoover.org

Hoover Institution Press Publication No. 445
Copyright © 1998 by the Board of Trustees of the
    Leland Stanford Junior University
All rights reserved. No part of this publication may be reproduced,
stored in a retrieval system, or transmitted in any form or by any
means, electronic, mechanical, photocopying, recording, or
otherwise, without written permission of the publisher.

Cover photo credit: © 1997 PhotoDisc, Inc.

First printing, 1998
13   12   11   10   09   08   07   06   9   8   7   6   5   4   3

Manufactured in the United States of America

The paper used in this publication meets the minimum requirements
of the American National Standard for Information Sciences—
Permanence of Paper for Printed Library Materials, ANSI Z39.48–1992.

Library of Congress Cataloging-in-Publication Data
What's gone wrong in America's classrooms / edited by Williamson M. Evers.
    p. cm. — (Hoover Institution Press publication ; no. 445)
    Includes bibliographical references and index.
    ISBN 0-8179-9532-3 (alk. paper)
    1. Education—United States. 2. School improvement programs—United States.
3. Progressive education—United States. 4. Learning by discovery—United
States. 5. Reading—United States. 6. Academic achievement—United States.
I. Evers, Williamson M., 1948– .
II. Series: Hoover Institution Press publication ; 445.
LA217.2.W528   1998
370'.973–dc21   98-16765
                                              CIP

Contents

Foreword

Many citizens think that Americans are spending more on primary and secondary education and getting less, that the impact of declining performance is falling disproportionately on the low-income and minority segments of society, and that America's children are falling behind the rest of the world's.

Hoover fellows continue to be involved in this dialogue and debate, among them Nobel laureate Milton Friedman, who proposed a school voucher system in his 1962 classic *Capitalism and Freedom*, and Terry Moe, who challenged the education establishment in *Politics, Markets, and America's Schools.*

During February 24–25, 1997, Hoover fellow Williamson M. Evers convened a conference at the Hoover Institution to examine how elementary and secondary students learn and how we teach them in the classroom. University professors, public officials, educational researchers, and veterans of classroom teaching addressed the relative merits of the progressive education pedagogy versus traditional teaching techniques. In the course of this two-day event, these experts addressed the teaching philosophies and methodologies of reading, spelling, and math as well as student performance within these disciplines.

This volume is a collection of papers selected from presentations made at the conference, supplemented by related essays on this topic. The conference agenda is included as an appendix.

We would like to thank the Bertha and John Garabedian Charitable Foundation, the Jaquelin Hume Foundation, the Koret Foundation, and the David and Lucille Packard Foundation for their generous financial support of the conference and this book. Furthermore, added support was available from Hoover's Program on American Institutions and Economic Performance, generously supported by numerous donors, including the Taube Family Foundation, the Koret Foundation, Joanne and Johan Blokker, and the Sarah Scaife Foundation.

Conferences at the Hoover Institution are possible only through the efforts of our dedicated staff; I especially want to thank Associate Director Richard Sousa, Joanne Fraser-Thompson, Teresa Judd, and Mary Beth Nikitin for their significant contributions. Patricia Baker, executive editor of the Hoover Press, and her colleagues are commended for their work in publishing this book. Finally, without the intellectual stimulus and organizational efforts of Williamson Evers, this project would not have been completed.

John Raisian
Director, Hoover Institution
January 1998

Williamson M. Evers

Introduction

Policymakers, journalists, parents, and taxpayers agree that the public schools in the United States need a major overhaul. The question is how to get at the schools' many problems.

The academic problems are serious. Student scores have gone down on standardized tests designed to predict general college-level ability. The gap between current scores and those of thirty years ago is so great that the testmakers have recentered the tests to reflect present-day low performance.

In the recent Third International Mathematics and Science Survey, American students placed below Bulgarian students. The United States is not on the bottom, but it is well below Singapore, Japan, and South Korea.

Some of these national problems are particularly acute in California, which is tied for last place (with Louisiana) in comparative evaluations of students' reading ability. California is also near the bottom on like assessments of students' mathematical ability.

There are, broadly speaking, two ways to get at these deficiencies. The first approach tries to break up or drastically reduce the public schools' monopoly features and their entanglement in the red tape of politically dictated regulations. It includes privatization, vouchers that could be used in public and private schools or only in public schools, charter schools, and dividing large districts into smaller ones. That approach might have an effect, but it is politically difficult to implement. Other more modest structural ideas (such as the current fashion of limited-authority school-site councils of parents, teachers, and administrators) are unlikely to have much of an effect.

The second approach—the focus of this book—aims at the classroom. Because we know that American students spend more time in the classroom than German or Japanese students, are assigned more homework than Japanese students, and watch no more television than Japanese students, perhaps current American classroom instruction is part of the problem.

Seeking educational reform through improving classroom instruction is compatible with seeking reform through structural change. But they are different.

Evidence about effective teaching practices should be useful to both public and private schools as they are organized today and if they undergo some dramatic structural reform in the future.

Today one point of view dominates schools of education, academic journals, government funding agencies, and private foundations. This dominant point of view is progressive education, or, as it is often called, *discovery learning*.

Because elementary and secondary education is a monopoly, it is unlike competitive industries in which information about consumer preferences is signaled by purchases of goods and services. In a competitive, private industry, sales information signals capitalist-entrepreneurs who make calculations and decisions about the production process. They try different ways to satisfy the consumer. If the Edsel doesn't sell, managers don't spend time fighting about the philosophy of automobilism. Instead, resources and people are transferred from Edsel production to products that, it is hoped, will satisfy consumers.

In education, however, when the public schools are doing a poor job, public school managers *do* spend time fighting over the philosophy of pedagogy. The rivalry in education is not over how best to satisfy the customer (the parent) but over who is to control the monopoly production process.

Off and on during much of the twentieth century, progressive education has held sway over the education industry. It enjoys such hegemony today and has since the early 1980s, when people educated in the 1960s came into positions of authority. Yet there is no reason to believe from the evidence that either discovery learning or its close relative, "teaching for self-esteem," actually boosts scholastic achievement. Indeed, California public schools have taught reading exclusively via the progressive approach called *whole language* for the past nine years. It has been a catastrophe.

Similarly, California schools have taught math via discovery learning since 1985 and more comprehensively since 1992. The decline in scores on the entry-level mathematics test given in California State Universities indicates that another catastrophe may well be in the making.

The Plan of the Book

This book begins with large topics. My essay is on the progressive education ideology of teaching. Bonnie Grossen's is on the need for research on what works and making sure that research is reliable.

After this treatment of general, broad issues, the next five essays look at particulars. The essays by Jack M. Fletcher and G. Reid Lyon and by Bill Honig concern reading instruction. Louisa Cook Moats's focus is on instruction in reading and spelling. Harold W. Stevenson's essay compares mathematics instruction in East Asia, Europe, and North America. Maureen DiMarco writes about testing.

Finally, E. D. Hirsch Jr. concludes the volume by revisiting the general issue of ideological policy versus research-based policy.

It might seem that mathematics receives short shrift since only Stevenson's essay is entirely on this topic. But many of the examples in the essays by Grossen, DiMarco, and Hirsch and in my own essay are drawn from mathematics instruction.

The Essays

My chapter, "From Progressive Education to Discovery Learning," says that progressive education has had its ups and downs in the twentieth century but is influential today in its incarnation as discovery learning. The essay points out that progressive education draws on ideas from the Romantic Era—that children can and should learn all things naturally, enticed by their curiosity into learning by doing or learning by problem solving.

Unfortunately, even progressive educationalists like John Dewey, who wanted children to learn serious content in a natural way, ended up giving higher priority to natural modes of instruction than to content. The difficulty is that when external standards of content are downplayed, progressive education turns into child centeredness without intellectual discipline.

Bonnie Grossen asks, "What Is Wrong with American Education?" Her answer is that education needs to become an applied science. Large changes in instructional practices should not just be based on plausible, clever ideas or even on small-scale or anecdotal research; large changes should be based on large-scale research. Grossen discusses the large-scale changeover to whole-language reading instruction in California and the nationwide changeover to discovery learning in mathematics instruction—both without support from large-scale research.

But the bulk of Grossen's chapter is an account of Project Follow-Through, a large-scale (more than $1 billion) comparative study of instructional practices. The data from Follow-Through (evaluating the performance of more than seventy thousand students) showed that structured, teacher-directed instruction had better academic results (and better results in terms of self-esteem) than child-centered, discovery-learning approaches. Yet educationalists have ignored the findings of Follow-Through, and the approaches that failed to boost scholastic achievement in the Follow-Through study are among the most popular in American education today. Grossen concludes that the teaching profession needs to become more like the medical profession—doing and paying attention to large-scale research.[1]

In "Reading: A Research-Based Approach," Jack M. Fletcher and G. Reid Lyon review in detail the thirty years of research (sponsored at the national level by the National Institute of Child Health and Human Development) on how children learn to read and why they fail to learn to read. Human speech is natural, the result of biological evolution; reading and writing are artificial, although they build on our natural capacities. To read, people have to first be aware of the separate sounds sometimes hidden in human speech (phonemic awareness). Then they must apply this awareness to print. Reading problems come primarily from being unable to recognize single words in print. In turn these problems stem from some people's difficulties in segmenting words and syllables into phonemes.

---

1. Grossen tends to think that structural reforms (such as privatization) are unlikely to produce educational improvements since many private schools now adopt unproven educational techniques. But bringing widespread competition into the sleepy educational industry would change its dynamics entirely, and performance would doubtless become much more important than it is now.

Most of Fletcher and Lyon's chapter is a painstaking discussion of what has been learned from each of the various studies of reading. They speak carefully and tentatively about what is known and what needs further study. But they recommend that children have explicit, systematic instruction in decoding and word recognition skills (learning the alphabet and its sounds, rhyming games to teach phonemic awareness, sounding out techniques, and so forth), not out of the context of the rest of reading but as part of a complete program that includes emphasis on comprehension, literature, and writing.

Bill Honig's chapter, "Preventing Failure in Early Reading Programs," draws a picture of a good program for teaching beginners to read, which he says has elements from both the whole-language approach and the skills approach.

A good reading program enables the student to recognize words and understand passages. Unfortunately, the whole-language movement emphasizes the importance of comprehension over decoding skills. But, Honig says, decoding skills allow the reader to puzzle out an unknown word and begin to add it to his brain's word list so that later he recognizes it automatically.

Readers can use cues from the context for comprehension—to ascertain vocabulary meaning, for sorting out ambiguities and subtleties, and to confirm word recognition in any particular case—but using context as a regular basis for figuring out a word is too slow and too unreliable. The mistake of the whole-language movement, according to Honig, was taking tools entirely appropriate for comprehension and insisting on them as the exclusive method for word recognition.

Some children pick up reading easily, but many need to be taught the alphabet explicitly, including the sounds that letters represent (phonemic awareness) and how to sound out words (phonics). These students then need practice with unpredictable but decodable text. Once students master the basics, they should be comfortable in a broad language-arts curriculum (informed by some of the findings of whole-language practitioners) that includes writing, reading good literature, and discussion. It is this combination, according to Honig, that constitutes a good reading program.

In "Spelling and Language Structure," Louisa Cook Moats says that for too long we have seen children taught to spell by guessing at letters or picturing the shape of words. The key to success in spelling is apprehending language structure. Good spellers are sensitive to language structure, bad spellers are not. Teachers can teach students about language structure, including the phonemic awareness that is part of good reading instruction. Students can also be taught how to take a word apart and how to remember a word and its components. Students should learn the meanings of a word and sometimes the historical reasons (rooted in the history of the language) why a word is spelled the way it is. If we can take words apart and understand and learn their make-up, we can readily spell 98 percent of the words in the English language.

Harold W. Stevenson begins his essay by affirming that there is "no likelihood" that American students will be "first in the world" in mathematics in the year 2000—a goal listed in the national Goals 2000 program and well known to American educators. The scores of American students are not low because some discrete group of poorly performing students pulls down the average (the whole range of American students is lower than that of East Asian students) or because other countries test only their best students (they don't). The explanation is that, in contrast to their Western counterparts, East Asian teachers know the contents of their math lessons thoroughly and are more effective in teaching that content.

American teachers are self-satisfied, according to Stevenson, and convinced that sensitivity is a more important teacher trait than clarity of presentation. Even though American teachers know that they should have well-thought-out lesson plans (especially in relating problems and problem-solving techniques to mathematical concepts), they don't have such lesson plans, and the American educational system wouldn't encourage or reward them if they did. Compounding the problems arising from inadequate teaching practices, American students (and parents) are self-satisfied and unconvinced that better efforts will yield better results. Stevenson concludes that the main problems with American math instruction lie not in inadequate financial support but in existing cultural attitudes. It will not be easy, he says, but these attitudes must change.

In "Measurement and Reform," Maureen DiMarco looks at testing—which can tell us about how a student (or school or teacher) is doing and which has a major influence on what teachers teach. First, she reviews the history of testing of California schoolchildren, looking especially at the recently deceased California Learning Assessment System (CLAS). She says that students taking the CLAS test were supposed to receive individual scores and that the scores were supposed to be comparable nationally and internationally. Those writing the CLAS test were supposed to include a balanced mix of multiple-choice and open-ended performance items, and these items were supposed to test students' knowledge of basic skills and their ability to apply those skills. The state educational bureaucracy and its consultants went to work devising the test, and none of what was supposed to happen, happened. DiMarco illustrates what went wrong in the CLAS test using the math part of the test.

Then DiMarco talks about the need for different kinds of tests for different purposes. Parents (in both private and public schools), taxpayers, and politicians want to measure results. Teachers, principals, district superintendents, and school boards want to know how the teaching process is going. These differing goals require different tests. Finally, DiMarco reminds us that school administrators are tempted to switch to a different test when the results on the test they are using are bad.

E. D. Hirsch Jr.'s chapter closes the book by returning to the themes in my and Bonnie Grossen's chapters. He focuses on the counterproductive effects of educational fads and ideologies and on the need to base policy on reliable research. He offers some rules of thumb for determining the scientific reliability of research. He asks us to take seriously what top researchers in scientific fields agree on. In the field of psychology, which is the key field for research on education, educationalists have embraced a "constructivist" ideology that is based on Romantic sentiment, not scientific facts. Radical constructivism is at odds with mainstream psychology.

This embrace of ideology rather than science has important consequences for educational practices. Hirsch provides examples from testing, mathematics instruction, and early childhood education. Many educationalists promote performance-based assessments, which research shows are the least reliable tests. Many educationalists discourage drill and practice in math instruction. But research shows that varied and repeated practice leading to rapid recall and automaticity is necessary to higher-order problem-solving skills in mathematics. Many educationalists propose withholding challenging content from young children on the grounds that they are not developmentally ready for it. But scientists have found no basis in fact for this practice, and educationalists who deny children opportunities to learn when their minds are most open are stunting their growth.

This book had its origins in a conference at the Hoover Institution at Stanford University in February 1997. Two of the authors in this book, G. Reid Lyon and E. D. Hirsch Jr., were unable to attend the conference but have contributed to this volume. Four people—John R. Anderson, professor of psychology at Carnegie Mellon University; Constance A. Jones, director of school programs for the Core Knowledge Foundation; Douglas Carnine of the National Center to Improve the Tools of Educators at the University of Oregon; and Jaime Escalante, mathematics instructor at Hiram Johnson High School in Sacramento—gave excellent presentations at the conference but are not represented in this volume.

My principal thanks go to those who presented papers at the conference or wrote chapters for this volume. I wish to thank Marion Joseph and Richard Askey for their advice on the conference program. Hoover Institution director John Raisian supported this project as part of a larger endeavor of enhancing policy research in the field of education. Associate Director Richard Sousa provided guidance during the preparations for the conference and the publication of this book. Executive Editor Patricia Baker oversaw the production of the book.

Finally, I wish to thank my wife, Leslie, and my children, Daniel and Pamela, who have all supported my interest in education.

Williamson M. Evers

From Progressive Education
to Discovery Learning

School reformers today are still trying to put into effect the turn-of-the-century progressive education ideas of John Dewey and others—often these days under the banner of "discovery learning." These ideas were largely misguided a hundred years ago, and they are largely misguided now.[1]

Public acceptance of progressive education has had its ups and downs. But progressive education has never gone away. It received widespread attention in the 1920s, when, in its purer form, it was concentrated in private rather than public schools. By the 1940s, in watered-down form, it became standard fare in schools of education and for public school curriculum planners. Progressive education went briefly out of fashion in the mid-1950s when life adjustment education became a national laughingstock.[2] But progressive education came back and is quite in-

1. I am indebted to Michael McKeown and Ze'ev Wurman, who reviewed an earlier draft of this essay and gave me the benefit of their advice.
2. Lawrence A. Cremin, *The Transformation of the School: Progressivism in American Education, 1876–1957* (New York: Alfred A. Knopf, 1961), pp. vii, 347; Diane Ravitch, *The Troubled Crusade: American Education, 1945–1980* (New York: Basic Books, 1983), pp. 64–80. The low point for progressive education in the twentieth century can be marked as 1957, when the magazine *Progressive Education* ceased publishing. *New York Times*, July 24, 1957.

fluential today in its contemporary incarnation of discovery learning.[3]

What is progressive education, where did it come from, when is it right and when is it wrong, and what is the alternative?

History and Substance of Progressive Education

Progressive education did not spring full grown from the head of Dewey or from the head of child-centered educationalist G. Stanley Hall.[4] It draws on earlier ideas from the Romantic era (in the early nineteenth century) in Western Europe. According to the Romantic notion, children can and should learn all things naturally. Learning new things easily excites children, according to the Romantic vision. Children are curious about everything. Children are like flowering plants. If they are just planted into good soil (a good learning environment), they will naturally grow and blossom.[5]

This Romantic-era view of children and of schooling had its origin in the writings of Jean-Jacques Rousseau (1712–78) and

3. Historian of education David B. Tyack writes that the "discovery approach" is "surely nothing new to those who have read Dewey's *Democracy and Education.*" Tyack, ed., *Turning Points in American Educational History* (Waltham, Mass.: Blaisdell, 1967), p. 323. See also John R. Anderson, Lynne M. Reder, and Herbert A. Simon, "Radical Constructivism and Cognitive Psychology," in Diane Ravitch, ed., *Brookings Papers on Education Policy, 1998* (Washington, D.C.: Brookings Institution Press, 1998), p. 236.

4. See G. E. Partridge, *Genetic Philosophy of Education: An Epitome of the Published Educational Writings of President G. Stanley Hall of Clark University* (New York: Sturgis & Walton, 1912), esp. pp. 72–87 (developmental appropriateness), 223–24 (child as natural learner), 226–27 (teaching practices), 260–65 (mathematics instruction), 310 (avoid drill and repetition; delay instruction in reading and writing until age ten); G. Stanley Hall, *Educational Problems*, 2 vols. (New York: D. Appleton, 1911).

5. Compare Paul Woodring, *Let's Talk Sense about Our Schools* (New York: McGraw-Hill, 1953), p. 65.

others. It is not so much that Rousseau himself was directly influential in America. But the Romantic era coincided with the time in which American intellectuals such as Ralph Waldo Emerson (1803–82) were shaping the beginnings of American culture. Hence it is the overall Romantic attitude toward learning, as E. D. Hirsch Jr. has shown in his book *The Schools We Need*,[6] that has been influential in the American approach to education.

Taking up Romantic themes that linked education to the maturation of the child, American philosopher John Dewey (1859–1952) taught, lectured, and wrote about how to change schools along the lines of his philosophical ideas about how we come to know things.[7] For some years, Dewey even had his own laboratory school affiliated with the University of Chicago. Discovery learning is a variant of progressive education, but it draws on

6. E. D. Hirsch Jr., *The Schools We Need and Why We Don't Have Them* (New York: Doubleday, 1996), pp. 74–79, 108–9. I am certainly not contending here that Dewey was a down-the-line philosophical adherent of Rousseau's thought. Rousseau and Dewey did, however, share a Romantic view of children's mentality and predilections.

7. I am concentrating on Dewey's instructional philosophy or pedagogy, not his political views on education.

Dewey was a non-Marxist socialist. He explicitly viewed public education as a "socialism of the intelligence and of the spirit" and thought this "socialism" was beyond questioning by reasonable people. "The School as a Social Center" (1902), in Sol Cohen, ed., *Education in the United States: A Documentary History*, vol. 4 (New York: Random House, 1974), p. 2229.

Dewey seems not to have considered that incentives in government agencies might be perverse or that people in the government or its public school system might be self-serving or abusive of power. On this aspect of Dewey, see Paul E. Peterson, "The New Politics of Choice," in Diane Ravitch and Maris A. Vinovskis, eds., *Learning from the Past: What History Teaches Us about School Reform* (Baltimore: Johns Hopkins University Press, 1995), pp. 220–22.

See also Bertrand Russell, "Reply to Criticism," in Paul Arthur Schlipp, ed., *The Philosophy of Bertrand Russell*, 3d ed. (New York: Tudor Publishing, 1951), pp. 731–34. Russell defends education in service of the individual and responds to the idea of education in service of the political community as advocated by progressive educator and Dewey disciple Boyd H. Bode. I am indebted to David Gordon for this reference.

ideas about the psychology of learning, in particular those of Jean Piaget (1896–1980).[8]

Dewey held that the child is a natural learner, with a native impulse to inquire, an "instinct of investigation."[9] Dewey celebrated the "native and unspoiled attitude of childhood, marked by ardent curiosity, fertile imagination, and love of experimental inquiry" and contended that this attitude was "very, very near" to scientific habits of mind.[10] He deplored classrooms where the "center of gravity" was in the teacher or in the textbooks or anywhere other than "the immediate instincts and activities of the child himself."[11]

Prominent progressive educators Harold O. Rugg and Ann Shumaker wrote that the new progressive sort of school they envisioned was to be devoted to "self-expression and maximum child growth, . . . [a place where children will be eager to go to school because] they dance; they sing . . . ; they model in clay and sand; they draw and paint, read and write, make up stories and dramatize them; they work in the garden" and so forth.[12]

Progressive education's emphasis on "the immediate instincts and activities of the child" made a lasting impression on the minds of Americans and is probably the most widely known

8. See Jean Piaget, *The Psychology of Intelligence* , trans. Malcolm Piercy and D. E. Berlyne (New York: Harcourt, Brace, 1950); Piaget, *The Child's Concept of Number,* trans. C. Gattegno and F. M. Hodgson (New York: Humanities Press, 1952); Piaget, Barbel Inhelder, and Alina Szeminska, *The Child's Concept of Geometry,* trans. E. A. Lunzer (New York: Basic Books, 1960).

9. John Dewey, *The Child and the Curriculum* and *The School and Society,* rev. ed. (Chicago: Phoenix Book published by University of Chicago Press, 1956), p. 44. See also Robert B. Westbrook, *John Dewey and American Democracy* (Ithaca, N.Y.: Cornell University Press, 1991), p. 98.

10. John Dewey, *How We Think* (1910), quoted in Westbrook, *John Dewey and American Democracy,* p. 169.

11. Dewey, *The Child and the Curriculum* and *The School and Society,* p. 34.

12. *The Child-Centered School* (Yonkers-on-Hudson, N.Y.: World Book, 1928), pp. vii, 2–5, quoted in Ravitch, *Troubled Crusade,* p. 50.

feature of progressive education. A famous cartoon of the 1950s shows a class of exhausted and bored students imploring, indeed begging their teacher, "Please, do we *have* to do what we feel like doing today?"[13] This cartoon, of course, somewhat misrepresents what Dewey wanted in the classroom. But it does accurately represent what other progressives, the advocates of child-centered education, have wanted.

The Progressive Agenda in Education

Dewey's disciples and other progressives also added some other items to the progressive pedagogic agenda:[14]

- All learning in school is to come through playing[15]

- Children's social and emotional development and psychological attitudes (self-concept, self-esteem, how well the child works with others) are to be given an overriding

13. David Holden, "John Dewey and His Aims of Education," in Mortimer Smith, ed., *The Public Schools in Crisis: Some Critical Essays* (Chicago: Regnery, 1956), p. 18; Woodring, *Let's Talk Sense*, p. 61; Westbrook, *John Dewey and American Democracy*, p. 503.

14. Compare list in Jacques Barzun, *Begin Here: The Forgotten Conditions of Teaching and Learning*, ed. Morris Philipson (Chicago: University of Chicago Press, 1991), pp. 46–47.

15. In 1913, the Los Angeles district superintendent wrote that "the principal business of the child is to play and to grow—not to read, write, spell, and cipher. These are incidental in importance. If they can be made part of the play, it is well to use them; if not they should be handled sparingly." Tyack, *Turning Points*, p. 321.

Dewey does say that there was intentionally "a kindergarten attitude" in instructional practices at all grade levels (ages four to fourteen) in the University of Chicago laboratory school. Dewey, *The Child and the Curriculum* and *The School and Society*, pp. 117–18. The phrase "kindergarten attitude" does not capture all that Dewey is proposing here, but it does show how readily Dewey's language lent itself to misinterpretation.

importance that has relegated accumulation of knowledge and intellectual training to a secondary role

- A high-school-as-supermarket curriculum, an approach in which core subjects are crowded out—in the words of critic Mortimer Smith: "hairdressing and embalming are just as important, if not a little more so, than history and philosophy"[16]

- Abolishing drudgery and hard work on the way to mastering a subject

- Abolishing competition among students

Dewey himself didn't advocate these things.[17] But many of Dewey's disciples and other progressives did.

Dewey: Teaching Subject Matter via Problem Solving

Dewey denounced the purist child-centered educators for wanting to discard subject matter and "guidance and direction" by teachers.[18] Dewey wanted teachers to direct children's activities instead of leaving them to "merely impulsive expression."[19]

16. Quoted in Ravitch, *Troubled Crusade*, p. 72. The Educational Policies Commission wrote: "There is no aristocracy of 'subjects.' . . . Mathematics and mechanics, art and agriculture, history and homemaking are all peers." *Education for All American Youth* (1944), quoted in Ravitch, *Troubled Crusade*, pp. 62–63.

17. Barzun, *Begin Here*, pp. 46–47.

18. *New Republic*, July 9, 1930, quoted in Woodring, *Let's Talk Sense*, pp. 60–61. Much of *Experience and Education* (1938) was a critique of the excesses of child-centered pedagogy. See also Westbrook, *John Dewey and American Democracy*, pp. 98–100, 168–69, 502–6; Ravitch, *Troubled Crusade*, pp. 58–59. One of Dewey's complaints about child-centered education is that it gave children's current desires a privileged status and would not produce children disposed to change the world politically when grown. Westbrook, p. 506.

19. Dewey, *The Child and the Curriculum* and *The School and Society*, pp. 36–37.

He wanted schools to teach the content of math, science, English, history, and vocational skills.[20]

Dewey sought to combine the child as natural learner with serious subject matter. He wanted to do this by taking the subject matter, which he viewed as abstracted and generalized from problems that humanity had undertaken to solve in the past, and destroying its abstract character. The subject matter would be turned into problems, which teachers would then pose to the students. Children in a progressive educational setting are always "re-inventing" and "re-devising" processes and procedures that mankind learned long ago.[21] In Dewey's words, "The child puts himself at the standpoint of the problems that have to be met and rediscovers . . . ways of meeting them.[22] . . . The fundamental necessity [is] leading the child to realize a problem as his own, so that he is self-induced to attend [to it] in order to find out its answer."[23] Rather than motivating students via grades or other rewards and punishments, Dewey wanted to motivate them by appealing to what he thought was their natural curiosity—by immersing them in situations filled with challenging or puzzling problems.[24]

Part of the appeal and initial plausibility of progressive edu-

20. Westbrook, *John Dewey and American Democracy*, pp. 104, 505. See also ibid., p. 169 n. 7, on the possible compatibility of Dewey's educational philosophy with E. D. Hirsch's idea of cultural literacy.

21. Dewey, *The Child and the Curriculum* and *The School and Society*, p. 21. Dewey carried this to absurd lengths. For example, at the University of Chicago laboratory school, he opposed allowing children who were learning to cook to follow recipes; they had to discover on their own what ingredients to use and in what proportions and how long and how hot to cook foods (ibid., p. 38). Dewey makes this out to be a science project. But his policy runs the risk of leaving quite a few children sick to their stomachs.

22. Dewey, *The Child and the Curriculum* and *The School and Society*, p. 108.

23. Ibid., p. 149.

24. Ibid., pp. 148–49. Westbrook, *John Dewey and American Democracy*, pp. 168–69. Dewey wanted the child to see why the skill was needed. Ibid., p. 102.

cation is that people intuitively recognize that not everything we learn in life comes from books or by proceeding logically through subject matter. We do learn much of what we learn in life "by doing." Much of what we learn in the way of social culture, we learn through informal apprenticeships. Where the progressives went wrong was when they decided that all learning—including learning what Dewey called "intellectual subject matter"—had to be "by doing."

Dewey said that all thinking is practical problem solving. Critics correctly point out that Dewey's formulation leaves out much of abstract reasoning and even scientific discovery.[25] But this formulation is certainly Dewey's main legacy to discovery learning today—a strong, almost exclusive emphasis on learning through problem solving. Yet Dewey's philosophical formulation—unjustified as philosophy—is also inconsistent with recent findings of cognitive psychology, as will be discussed below in the section on discovery learning.

Demands on Progressive Teachers

What Dewey was asking teachers to do is actually quite difficult to accomplish. Since progressive educationalists and discovery learning educationalists ask teachers to discard or downplay textbooks and traditional teaching practices in favor of hands-on projects, manipulatives, and nonroutine problems, teachers who successfully teach in this style have to be quite creative and have in-depth knowledge of the subject matter.[26] You cannot take a nonroutine math problem and get at the many

25. Brand Blanshard, chap. 10, "Pragmatism and Thought," in Blanshard, *The Nature of Thought*, vol. 1 (London: George Allen & Unwin, 1939), pp. 341–93.

26. Compare Ravitch, *Troubled Crusade*, p. 47.

ways to solve it and explain the underlying mathematical concepts if you do not know what you are talking about.[27]

For this reason proponents of progressive education and discovery learning put particular stress on extensive (and expensive) retraining of teachers in progressive methods. But it is not surprising that critics and skeptics have often said that it would take someone as knowledgeable and skilled in teaching as John Dewey in every classroom for progressive education to work.[28]

Lawrence A. Cremin, a historian of American education, writes:

> What the progressives [prescribed] made inordinate demands on the teacher's time and ability. "Integrated studies" required familiarity with a fantastic range of knowledge and teaching materials; while the commitment to build upon student needs and interests demanded extraordinary feats of pedagogical ingenuity. In the hands of first-rate instructors, the [progressive] innovations worked wonders; in the hands of too many average teachers, however, they led to chaos. Like the proverbial little girl with the curl right in the middle of her forehead, progressive

27. There is good reason to doubt that American teachers are familiar with explaining math concepts. According to the Third International Mathematics and Science Study (TIMSS), 95 percent of American math teachers say they are aware of the math reform program of the National Council of Teachers of Mathematics (which includes teaching of concepts as its centerpiece) and almost 75 percent say they have implemented the program in their classes. But all the evidence in TIMSS (videos, textbooks, etc.) shows that mathematics is not being taught in depth in America, and the TIMSS videos of American classrooms show that math concepts are almost totally neglected. Lois Peak et al., *Pursuing Excellence: A Study of U.S. Eighth-Grade Mathematics and Science Teaching, Learning, Curriculum, and Achievement in International Context*, U.S. Department of Education, National Center for Educational Statistics (Washington, D.C.: U.S. Government Printing Office, 1996), pp. 42–47. See also Steve Baldwin "Math Movement Robs Generation of Basic Skills," *San Diego Union Tribune*, December 22, 1996.

28. See, for example, Albert Lynd, *Quackery in the Public Schools* (Boston: Little, Brown, 1953), p. 208.

education done well was very good indeed; done badly, it was abominable—worse, perhaps, than the formalism it had sought to replace.[29]

It should be noted that "guided" discovery learning with tried-and-true, carefully scripted lesson plans (as found in Japan) is not as perilous as pure discovery learning and could fare better in the hands of average teachers.

Subject Matter and Children's Impulses: Breakdown of the Synthesis

Although Dewey wanted to have students naturally discover important subject matter through solving problems, his synthesis of the child as natural learner and the learning of serious subject matter tends to break down whenever a conflict between the two arises. Dewey himself always emphasized the natural impulses of the child more than intellectual training and discipline.[30] He explicitly says that the "primary root" of "all educational activity" is not the presentation and mastery of subject material, but rather the instinctive, impulsive attitudes and activities of the child.[31] His even more child-centered disciples,

29. Cremin, *Transformation of the School*, pp. 348–49.

30. Dewey consistently disparaged any style of instruction "which appeals for the most part simply to the intellectual aspect of our natures" and without fail supported practices that stressed the human impulses "to make, to do, to create, to produce." Dewey, *The Child and the Curriculum* and *The School and Society*, p. 26. See also pp. 17, 25–26, 101–2; and Mortimer Smith, *And Madly Teach: A Layman Looks at Public School Education* (Chicago: Regnery, 1949), p. 17.

31. Dewey, *The Child and the Curriculum* and *The School and Society*, p. 117. Similarly, "The Principles of Progressive Education" of the Progressive Education Association state that "[school records] should . . . serve to focus the attention of the teacher on the all-important work of development rather than on simply teaching subject matter." *Progressive Education: A Quarterly Review of the Newer Tendencies in Education* 1 (April 1924): 1.

such as William Heard Kilpatrick, just took Dewey's own emphasis further.[32] Because Dewey would not give priority to learning the subject matter, he bequeathed his successors an approach to educational reform that didn't have within itself a nonsense detector. Nothing clearly excluded or ruled out such notions as all schoolwork should be play (or, to put it another way, all schoolwork should be exciting, fun, hands-on projects, undertaken without regard to whether they improve scholastic achievement).

Indeed, in the hands of Dewey's disciples, such notions seemed a natural extension and reasonable application of Dewey's philosophy. His disciples could dismiss one element after another of serious subject matter all too easily. The secretary of the Progressive Education Association could unblushingly write, "Consider cube root! Whoever heard of it outside the textbook? What child wants to? Why should he?"[33]

In sum, progressive education—as given to us by Dewey and other progressives and interpreted by their disciples—implies learning almost entirely through problem solving. It can all too easily mean a disdain for bookish, systematic intellectual study. It encourages clothing Romantic sentimentality in behavioral science jargon. The child-centered variant of progressive education diminishes accountability; it relieves teachers from the duty of getting through the subject and getting the subject matter into the child's head.[34] The teacher can just say: We teach the child, not the subject matter. It easily glides over into giving overriding importance to the child's emotional sentiments and affect.

32. For a hilarious account of Kilpatrick's pedagogic thought, see Lynd, *Quackery in the Public Schools*, chap. 9, "The World of Professor Kilpatrick," pp. 212–54.
33. Morton Snyder, "What Is Progressive Education?" (1927), in Cohen, *Education in the United States*, vol. 4, p. 2447.
34. Compare Smith, *And Madly Teach*, p. 23.

To the extent that progressive education (despite the strictures of Dewey) has demoted subject matter, it has done a serious disservice to education. Albert Lynd put it eloquently when he said,

> There is more wisdom in the "subject matter" of mathematics, of literature, of history, than in any teacher or body of teachers, however wise. In depreciating "subject matter" the Educationist is removing from the curriculum that which even the worst teacher can only partially spoil; when a poor teacher teaches without it, everything may be spoiled.[35]

Discovery Learning

The basic idea of discovery learning is that people can only learn things and understand them (or, in a more moderate version, can best learn things and understand them) when they discover them for themselves. Discovery learning calls for virtually the same instructional practices as John Dewey's—the idea that students should be put in a situation where they face some problem that is well known to educators but not to the students, and then the students are to reinvent solutions to the problem. Whereas John Dewey backed his progressive pedagogy with philosophical ideas about what truth is and what happens when we think, discovery learning relies for its justification on psychological theories about learning ("radical constructivism") and about the maturation of children's mental faculties ("developmental appropriateness").

---

35. Lynd, *Quackery in the Public Schools*, pp. 69–70.

Constructivism

Our minds do not photograph or passively mirror reality after we see or experience something.[36] Our minds interpret new perceptual input in light of what we already know and anticipate. This is widely accepted in the psychology profession.[37]

Radical constructivists believe that constructivist learning theory unequivocally dictates a discovery learning teaching style. They begin by saying that all children are "active learners." So far, so good: that learning is an active process is not controversial.

The leap that radical constructivists then make is saying that constructive learning theory means that the best way to learn is via the discovery approach: experiments, real-world problem solving, and hands-on projects. But, in fact, constructivist learning theory, properly understood, does not dictate how to teach.

The radical constructivists then go on to say that all children are in a position to construct (via discovery) complex bodies of intellectual knowledge. If, for example, children are to fully grasp mathematics, say the radical constructivists, they must rediscover its concepts on their own. And, with a teacher as a "facilitator," according to the radical constructivists, "it is possible

36. Recognizing the active role of mental processes (i.e., psychological construction) does not rule out a realist theory of what we know and how we know it. See Susan Haack, *Evidence and Inquiry: Toward Reconstruction in Epistemology* (Oxford, Eng.: Blackwell, 1993); David Kelley, *The Evidence of the Senses: A Realist Theory of Perception* (Baton Rouge: Louisiana State University Press, 1986). Realists would, however, rather not use the term *construction* to describe what goes on.

37. Anderson et al., "Radical Constructivism and Cognitive Psychology," p. 232; Hirsch, *The Schools We Need*, pp. 133–34.

for students to construct for themselves the mathematical practices that, historically, took several thousand years to evolve."[38]

It is true that all learning (even rote memorization) takes place via construction. But, contrary to the view of the radical constructivists, sometimes things are best learned through projects, sometimes through rote memorization, sometimes through problem solving, and sometimes through lectures or reading books. How best to learn something is an empirical question.[39]

Learning through projects and problems can be successful. But it has its drawbacks and pitfalls. Students of mathematics can take a long time (weeks) using the discovery process to come up with the concept of "slope." A teacher can explain it directly to the students much more quickly.[40]

Construction can lead to mistaken ideas. Let us take a young child who has memorized the Christmas carol "Silent Night." Now this child doesn't know about some matters, so he thinks "round yon Virgin" is "round John Version"—a chubby, rotund person. He has memorized the carol. He has constructed knowledge, but his "knowledge" includes misunderstandings.[41]

A complex problem often requires drawing on several skills.

---

38. P. Cobb, E. Yackel, and T. Wood, "A Constructivist Alternative to Representational View of Mind in Mathematics Education" (1992), quoted in David C. Geary, *Children's Mathematical Development: Research and Practical Applications* (Washington, D.C.: American Psychological Association, 1994), p. 263; Geary, "Reflections of Evolution and Culture in Children's Cognition: Implications for Mathematical Development and Instruction," *American Psychologist* 50, no. 1 (January 1995): 31.

39. Anderson et al., "Radical Constructivism and Cognitive Psychology," pp. 237, 238. A related paper is John R. Anderson, Lynne M. Reder, and Herbert A. Simon, "Applications and Misapplications of Cognitive Psychology to Mathematics Education," April 21, 1995. http://sands.psy.cmu.edu/personal/ja/misapplied.html/

40. Compare Anderson et al., "Radical Constructivism and Cognitive Psychology," p. 240.

41. Compare Hirsch, *The Schools We Need*, p. 234.

If a student has not already mastered most of these skills, having to use all of them in the same problem can be too much to handle. In contrast, if the student has already mastered most of these skills, having to use them would be a waste of time, when the student could be concentrating on skills he has not yet mastered.[42]

The project approach and the problem-centered approach take more time than exposition, lecturing, or other forms of direct instruction and are prone to students constructing the wrong thing in their minds—constructing "round John Versions."

That is why good mathematical instruction aimed at conceptual understanding (for example, instruction as done in Japan) uses carefully chosen problems. A carefully worked-out lesson plan covers most expected contingencies. The students explain and defend their work under the close guidance and supervision of the teacher, who knows the subject in depth, who provides closure to each lesson, and who makes sure students see what the goal of each lesson was.[43] Such instruction in Japan is by no means pure student self-discovery. It is by no means every child his own Archimedes, his own Pythagoras.

Developmental Appropriateness

The term *developmental appropriateness* refers to the idea that even beyond the crib and toddler stage, children's mental faculties are unfolding at a pace that must not be rushed or hurried. That unfolding should proceed at a "natural" rate. Presenting an

42. Anderson et al., "Radical Constructivism and Cognitive Psychology," p. 241.

43. Harold W. Stevenson and James W. Stigler, *The Learning Gap: Why Our Schools Are Failing and What We Can Learn from Japanese and Chinese Education* (New York: Simon & Schuster, 1992), p. 179; Geary, *Children's Mathematical Development*, pp. 270–71.

intellectual challenge that is "inappropriate" will be ineffectual or even harmful to the child, according to this theory.[44]

Proponents of developmentally appropriate instruction often say that the work of psychologist Jean Piaget supplies scientific support for their educational theories. Piaget portrays children as going through stages of cognitive development. Unfortunately for proponents of developmentally appropriate instruction, the facts do not support Piaget's picture of stages. Most academic psychologists now working in this field would say that cognitive development is gradual, continuous, and cumulative.[45]

Psychologist David C. Geary[46] has brought together findings that help us see where the idea of "developmental appropriateness" goes astray. A certain few primary cognitive abilities, such as oral language, fine motor skills, play, and rudimentary conceptual understanding, we have naturally. They are programmed into us via genetics and the evolutionary mechanism of natural selection. They unfold at a natural tempo. Everything else—while sometimes built on or dependent on these primary abilities—is "unnatural." There is no natural tempo for developing secondary abilities—they have to be taught or acquired. Thus, almost all of what you hear from professional educators about not "hurrying" the child, waiting until the student is "developmentally ready," is wrong. Indeed it is has two pernicious effects: it discourages accelerated learning at an early age when the brain is open to it, and it removes accountability for teachers

44. See J. E. Stone, "Developmentalism: An Obscure but Pervasive Restriction on Educational Improvement," *Education Policy Analysis Archives* 4, no. 8 (April 21, 1996). http://olam.ed.asu.edu/epaa/v4n8.html.

45. Anderson et al., "Radical Constructivism and Cognitive Psychology," pp. 235, 251. See also Geary, *Children's Mathematical Development*, pp. 81–86.

46. Geary, *Children's Mathematical Development*, esp. chap. 8; Geary, "Reflections of Evolution and Culture," pp. 24–37.

and students.[47] What is in reality a teacher's failure to teach properly or a student's failure to put the effort in that is needed to learn can be excused as a case in which the student was not yet "ready to learn."

Furthermore, Geary points out that in math, for example, skills and facts (except at the earliest, infant-in-the-crib level of primitive number sense) are not primary cognitive abilities.[48] Students need to learn facts and skills through drill and practice. Students need to practice math skills until they are fluent in their use (just as phonics has to become automatic for good readers). In math, fluency and automaticity are needed to free the brain to concentrate on conceptual understanding. In Japan, for example, students have take-home workbooks and go to after-school tutoring programs to become automatic at math skills.[49] Classtime can then concentrate on alternative ways to solve problems.

Direct Instruction

Progressivism has always had its critics. William C. Bagley, of the Teachers College at Columbia—itself the center and stronghold of progressivism—said in 1934 that replacing "systematic and sequential learning" and putting in its place "activities" would "defeat the most important ends of education in democracy," specifically, the objective of attaining "as high a level

47. It can also lead to hesitancy or even paralysis on the part of the teacher, who often cannot ascertain what "stage" a child is in. See Stone, "Developmentalism."

48. Geary, "Reflections of Evolution and Culture," p. 32.

49. "Japanese experts report that instruction in mathematics *juku* (afterschool programs) focuses more on review and practice of basic skills than is typical of the Japanese classroom." Lois Peak et al., *Pursuing Excellence*, p. 64. See also Stevenson and Stigler, *Learning Gap*, pp. 56, 67.

of common culture as possible."[50] There is an alternative to the progressive approach: direct instruction or explicit teaching.[51] Direct instruction receives support from recent findings in cognitive psychology: although children do naturally pick up what Geary calls "primary cognitive abilities" (such as spoken language and fine motor skills) without being taught, children are born ignorant and for most skills and knowledge ("secondary cognitive abilities") need to be explicitly taught by people who know the subject.[52] Teachers are expected to know more than students and should seek to transmit that knowledge. Teachers should not respond to all questions from students in class (as some discovery learning teachers do) with: "What do you think?"

Subject matter often has an inherent internal logic and can be organized on a ladder of increasing difficulty and complexity— a ladder of learning, if you will. Some material has to be mastered before one can go on to the next step. Much subject matter has this hierarchical character, and students have to learn it step by step.

Most children are not "naturally curious" about learning the multiplication tables or the long-division algorithm or the rigor of the scientific method.[53] Children have to learn them through explicit guidance and through drill and practice.[54] Disciplined

50. Quoted in Ravitch, *Troubled Crusade*, p. 58.
51. For further elaboration, see Bonnie Grossen, "What Is Wrong with American Education," in this volume.
52. Geary, *Children's Mathematical Development*; Geary, "Reflections of Evolution and Culture."
53. "The motivation to acquire complex biologically secondary cognitive abilities is based on the requirements of the larger society and not on the inherent interests of children." Geary, "Reflections of Evolution and Culture," p. 28.
54. "Nothing flies more in the face of the last 20 years of research than the assertion that practice is bad. . . . By denying the critical role of practice, one is denying children the very thing they need to achieve real competence." Anderson et al., "Radical Constructivism and Cognitive Psychology," p. 241. See also

study and books and bookish things are needed to banish ignorance and instill knowledge. To ascertain whether students have mastered the material, students need to take tests, do homework, and write reports that are their own individual work. They likewise need to respond in class individually (and not just as a representative of a cooperative learning group) to questions posed by the teacher.

Direct instruction should not exclude projects, field trips, group work, or a student explaining at length in class (under guidance from the teacher) how the student solved a problem. But the nonprogressive educationalist would strictly subordinate efforts to enlist student interest and the use of motivational techniques to the task of getting the student to learn the subject matter.

Conclusion

There are some good things about progressivism and discovery learning: progressive educators seek to motivate the student to take an interest in his or her studies; they refuse to rely exclusively on recitation, memorization, textbooks, and instilling passivity.[55] In the 1890s, before progressivism, exclusive reliance on these methods was standard instructional practice.[56]

At the same time, we do know that students have to master— to learn so that they are automatic—skills in reading, spelling, and mathematical facts and operations. We know that the need to acquire skills and learn facts goes beyond the 3-R fundamen-

---

Geary, *Children's Mathematical Development,* pp. 265–66, 269–70; Geary, "Reflections of Evolution and Culture," p. 27, 32–33.

55. Compare, Ravitch, *Troubled Crusade,* p. 51.

56. Joseph C. Rice, *The Public School System of the United States* (New York: Century Company, 1893).

tals and does not end in third grade with mastery of the multiplication tables. The need is ongoing—continuing through calculus and beyond in math and continuing through college-level reading and writing in English.

In the culturally important academic subjects—math, science, history and geography, foreign languages, literature, and the arts—curriculum planners can and should organize a curriculum that emphasizes content. Education in these subjects should be cumulative and sequential, with each year's study building on what has been learned previously. Curriculum planners, textbook writers, and teachers should not ignore or discard the tools, terminology, or methods that practitioners have historically used in academic disciplines. These tools and methods, along with the knowledge that practitioners have gained over time by using them, are in fact what define those disciplines.

We know that to attain advanced conceptual understanding in all subjects, explicit teaching is necessary. Conceptual understanding does not come without the hard work of studying a subject for a long time and in depth. The teacher needs to guide the student throughout and often to impart knowledge directly.

If teachers keep these things in mind, they can and should use large components of problem solving and applications in teaching and, certainly as well, individual or group projects. Teachers can make use of empirical findings about how best to teach subject matter without abandoning or neglecting the principle that knowledge in intellectual subject areas is connected by an inner logic.

The complaint of the fair-minded critics is not that there is nothing good in progressivism but that the progressive educators decline to look at the results of their methods.[57] Instead they

---

57. To some extent, the progressives' neglect of attention to quantitative

elevated those methods into a object of near-religious veneration and stressed method at the expense of knowledge of the subject matter.

Mortimer Smith, an outspoken but fair-minded critic, offers this balanced assessment of progressive education together with words of caution to proponents of direct instruction:

> In his zeal for the tried and true, the traditionalist should not overlook the many sensible aids to teaching and some of the sound guiding principles undoubtedly contained in progressive education. It is enough to point out that the movement has had a tendency to erect methods into dogmas with the unfortunate result that the process of learning overshadows the content to be learned.[58]

---

results was justified by Dewey:

> Quality of activity and of consequence is more important for the teacher than any quantitative element. If this fact prevents the development of a certain kind of science [the science of education], it may be unfortunate. But the educator cannot sit down and wait until there are methods by which quality may be reduced to quantity; he must operate here and now. If he can organize his qualitative processes and results into some connected intellectual form, he is really advancing scientific method much more than if, ignoring what is actually most important, he devotes his energies to such unimportant by-products as may now be measured. "Progressive Education and the Science of Education," (1928) in Cohen, vol. 4 *Education in the United States*, p. 2458.

58. Smith, *And Madly Teach*, pp. 20–21.

Bonnie Grossen

What Is Wrong with American Education?

The American public is growing increasingly impatient with public education. A recent Gallup poll documented that, for the first time ever, more than one-third of the American public is willing to spend public dollars for private schooling (Lawton 1996). The public disappointment with American education seems to stem from education's inability to produce learning comparable to what other nations produce. The American public is used to being first in the world in business, medicine, technology, agriculture, and so on. A nation so competitive in other areas should be equally competitive in education. Why is it not?

The education profession in America differs from other highly successful professions in one very significant way. Most other professions ensure to some extent that the procedures shared across the profession actually work to increase the success of all members of the profession. To ensure that they work, procedures are first tested in some way. These shared procedures form the professional knowledge base of the profession. New procedures come into the professional knowledge base only if they have been shown to yield better results than the old procedures they replace. The testing process effective professions use is based on the scientific method, the most dependable method for constructing new knowledge. By using the scientific method in the fields of medicine, engineering, agriculture, bricklaying, business, marketing, and so on to identify procedures over time that are effective, these professions become more productive. More lives are saved in medicine. More food per farmer is produced. Chimneys are built faster. Businesses are more productive, advertising becomes more effective, and so on.

Education is an unfortunate exception to this pattern of professional behavior. Teaching procedures are often widely disseminated without any evidence that the procedures work. This is not accidental. Many educational leaders explicitly and vehemently reject the scientific method as a means for identifying procedures that could work well for all the various members of the education profession.

Table 1 contrasts education with other professions that use a scientific process for identifying new knowledge. In other non-education professions, knowledge must pass through three levels of research before being accepted into the professional canon. Level-1 research can be any kind of activity that results in a new

TABLE 1
Using the Scientific Method to Form New Knowledge

Scientific Method	Education
Level 1. Develop a hypothesis through informal observation.	Theory building.
Level 2. Test the hypothesis by formally attempting to disprove it. Analyze the data to determine the truth of the hypothesis.	Test the theory on a small scale.
Level 3. Peer review, replication of the experiment, large-scale or long-term follow-up studies or both.	Replicate the results in large-scale studies and school district–wide implementations.

idea. For example, level-1 research can involve gathering data to describe a problem or anecdotally noting some relationship. Level-1 research results in a hypothesis. The fact that someone came up with a new idea (a hypothesis) does not immediately justify the adoption of that idea by the profession.

The next step is to try out the idea to see if it is an improvement. Only if it works better than the procedure it replaces should it be adopted by the profession. This kind of evidence requires comparative experimental research: level-2 and then level-3 research. Level-2 research is done on a small scale; level-3 research is done on a larger scale. Small-scale level-2 testing is necessary to reduce the risk in case the procedure does not work as well as expected in the larger-scale tests.

Once the procedure passes the small-scale tests of level 2, it moves on to level 3. The large-scale tests of level 3 are necessary to see if the procedure works consistently across various members of the profession in various circumstances. Only after a procedure has passed this level-3 test does it pass into the shared professional canon in other professions.

However, education does not build knowledge this way. Generally, new procedures are widely shared across the profession with only weak level-1 support at best (Ellis and Fouts 1993, 1994). Someone theorizes that a new procedure might be better than an old one, finds access to a powerful means for dissemination, and that procedure quickly becomes a fad widely disseminated without any further testing of the hypothesis. For example, research data that whole-language advocates frequently cited was that children learn oral language naturally. And clearly the data show that virtually all children learn to speak without any systematic instruction at all. This level-1 research is "true." But those data do not support a recommendation that teachers use whole-language instructional practices.

No teaching recommendation has a research base until the

procedure has been shown to have better results than the practice it intends to replace. It is misleading to say that studies of children's oral-language acquisition provide a research base for whole-language instruction because these studies did not evaluate the effects of whole-language instruction on reading acquisition. The first experimental test of this hypothesis was conducted as a high-risk nationwide experiment, and, unfortunately, the hypothesis proved wrong. Level-2 and level-3 research are necessary to eliminate risk. Unfortunately, level-2 and level-3 research are especially rare in education.

Project Follow-Through—Level-3 Research

Although level-3 education research has been rare, it has occurred. Project Follow-Through—the largest, most expensive research study in the history of education—is a prime example.

Follow-Through began in 1967 as part of President Lyndon Johnson's war on poverty and continued to receive funding until the summer of 1995. A massive effort to break the cycle of poverty through better education, it affected more than seventy thousand children a year in more than 180 schools and cost taxpayers more than $1 billion, unadjusted for inflation. Its goal was to identify teaching methods that could raise the level of performance of children in America's most economically deprived schools from the twentieth percentile (the normal level of performance for children in poverty) up to the fiftieth percentile (the level of mainstream America).

Two independent agencies worked on the evaluation of the teaching methods including in Project Follow-Through using various measures of self-esteem and academic achievement. Figure 1 shows the mean national academic achievement levels of children who were in the same program from grades kindergarten to grade 3, as measured by the Metropolitan Achievement

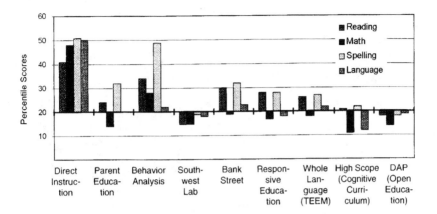

Figure 1. Graphic Representation of Achievement Data.

Test (MAT). The baseline in figure 1 is set at the twentieth percentile. When the bars go above this line, children's academic performance levels have climbed above what would be considered normal. When the bars go down, the children's performance was hindered by the model; that is, the children learned less than they would have without the model. As the graph indicates, only one model resulted in achievement near the fiftieth percentile, the target. The scores of children taught using the other models were significantly lower, often below the twentieth percentile.

The performance of each Follow-Through school was also compared with a non-Follow-Through school in the areas of academic performance, cognitive ability (the ability to learn how to learn), and measures of self-esteem. Figure 2 graphically displays how often this comparison was favorable for the particular Follow-Through model. When the bars go above the line, the models resulted in better scores more often than the comparison schools. When the bars go below the line, the Follow-Through models resulted in lower scores than the comparison schools.

Abt Associates, the independent group who analyzed the

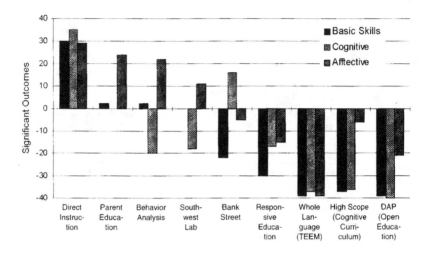

Figure 2.   Comparison of Outcomes across Follow-Through Models. 0 = No difference between the Follow-Through model and the comparison group.

data, found that the most popular child-centered models resulted in more negative outcomes than positive ones (Stebbins, St. Pierre, Proper, Anderson, and Cerva 1977). Abt Associates further noted that the most surprising outcome was that the Direct Instruction model had the best outcomes for self-esteem (Bock, Stebbins, and Proper 1977). The models that had improved self-esteem as their primary goal often had more-negative outcomes, even on the self-esteem measures. The Direct Instruction model did not target self-esteem as a goal. However, the sponsors predicted that, by targeting academic success and engineering the instruction so that students were highly successful each step of the way, self-esteem would result. As figure 2 shows, these predictions were accurate.

Most analysts of the Follow-Through evaluation data concluded that structured, teacher-directed instruction resulted in stronger academic outcomes than the popular child-centered models (Adams and Engelmann 1996; Bereiter and Kurland

1981; Kennedy 1978; Lindsley 1992; McDaniels 1975; Stebbins, St. Pierre, Proper, Anderson, and Cerva 1977).

> The two high-scoring models according to our analysis are Direct Instruction and Behavior Analysis; the two low-scoring are EDC Open Education and Responsive Education. If there is some clear meaning to Follow Through results, it ought to emerge from a comparison of these two pairs of models. On the one hand, distinctive characteristics of the first pair are easy to name: sponsors of both the Direct Instruction and Behavior Analysis models call their approaches "behavioral" and "structured" and both give a high priority to the three Rs. EDC and Responsive Education, on the other hand, are avowedly "child-centered." Although most other Follow Through models could also claim to be child-centered, these two are perhaps most militantly so and most opposed to what Direct Instruction and Behavior Analysis stand for. (Bereiter and Kurland 1981, 16–17)

Bereiter and Kurland (1981) further point out an aspect of the teacher-directed models that seemed to account for the higher achievement scores:

> Child-centered approaches rely almost exclusively on a form of instruction that . . . may be called *relevant activity*. . . . The instructional approaches used in Direct Instruction and Behavior Analysis reflect years of analysis and experimentation devoted to finding ways of going beyond relevant activity to forms of instruction that get more directly at cognitive skills and strategies. This effort has been successful in some areas, not so successful in others, but the effort goes on. Meanwhile, child-centered approaches have tended to fixate on the primitive, relevant-activities form of instruction for *all* their instructional objectives. (Bereiter and Kurland 1981, 20)

Overall, the learning and self-esteem of children of poverty were hampered by nondirective methods, methods that claimed to be "progressive" in their ideology. Ironically, these so-called progressive models had retrograde efects.

We cannot say from a comparative study such as Follow-Through that the one successful model is the only one that could be effective. Many alternative instructional models were not tested. How well these might have compared is not known. However, we have learned something about what was ineffective. Most of the models were "child centered," and the more vehemently "child centered" the model was, the poorer the results were. Thus, what we should have learned from the Follow-Through study was that child-centered instruction does not work well with children of poverty.

Despite this, the three lowest-scoring models in the Abt analysis, those that had the most negative outcomes (figure 2), are widely promoted today. The model with the most negative outcomes, the Open Education model, is the British infant and primary school model that is promoted today by the National Association for the Education of Young Children (NAEYC) under the new name, *developmentally appropriate practices.* NAEYC has successfully lobbied for a legislative mandate of these practices in several states. The cognitively oriented curriculum was High/Scope, one of the most widely adopted preschool models in America. Tucson Early Education Model (TEEM) was a language experience approach for reading instruction called *whole language.*

What Happened Next?

Before the final evaluation was published, the Ford Foundation funded an evaluation of the evaluation. That widely read critique by House, Glass, McLean, and Walker, published in 1978 by the *Harvard Educational Review,* raised questions about the design of Follow-Through, about the statistical methodology used by the independent evaluator, Abt, and about the appropriateness and accuracy of some of the self-esteem measures. However, the critique also included a reanalysis of the academic achievement data using different statistical methods. These results confirmed Abt Associates' academic ranking of Direct Instruction: It was by far the most successful of the Follow-Through models. The critique went on to endorse the MAT as a sound assessment of academic achievement in the early elementary grades, describing the test as "a technically sound instrument—highly reliable, well-normed, largely free of practical or conceptual flaws" (p. 138).

This agreement over Follow-Through's academic results wasn't emphasized during the initial debate, however—perhaps because House and his colleagues (as well as many others) believed that the primary significance of Follow-Through was as a *social*, not an educational, experiment. For the authors of the critique, "What model works best?"—the question of greatest interest to parents and teachers—was a question that Follow-Through should never have asked and Abt should never have attempted to answer.

Whatever the reasons, the result was that many nonacademic followers of the debate were left with the impression that Follow-Through had been completely discredited. Today, few teachers and parents know anything about Follow-Through, its findings, or the ongoing dispute over whether this or other forms of scientific inquiry should be attempted in the field of education.

In a 1981 report published by the National Institute of Education, the predecessor of the U.S. Department of Education's Office of Educational Research and Improvement (OERI), Glass and Camilli took issue with Follow-Through for even attempting to use scientific research to find solutions to educational problems. Level-2 and level-3 educational research, they argued, is immaterial, even to educators:

> The audience for Follow Through evaluations is an audience of teachers. This audience does not need the statistical findings of experiments when deciding how best to educate children. They decide such matters on the basis of complicated public and private understandings, beliefs, motives and wishes. They have the right and good reasons so to decide. (ERIC abstract ED244738, p. 21)

Unfortunately, this kind of thinking denies a scientific basis for education and opens the door to faddism and the revitalization of the same models that failed in the Follow-Through evaluation. Nothing was done to the Open Education model to make it more effective in its reincarnation as *developmentally appropriate practices*. Whole language is fundamentally the same as the language experience approach. High/Scope still advocates play time over academics.

From a logical standpoint, one cannot use level-1 research to overturn level-3 research. To claim that the poorest-performing models in Follow-Through are now research-based in the 1990s requires successful demonstrations at level 3. (Even level 2 might provide some evidence.) If such demonstrations were achieved and were more recent than the Follow-Through evaluation, then we could say that the Follow-Through data no longer hold or that the models have been improved.

The National Association for the Education of Young Children and Developmentally Appropriate Practices

In the mid-1980s, the National Association for the Education of Young Children (NAEYC) convened a committee to define the best practices for teachers. These were called *developmentally appropriate practices* (DAP). Johnson and McChesney Johnson (1992), who served on the NAEYC committees and who advocate DAP, described the purpose of these committee meetings as follows: "DAP was born from meetings of the NAEYC in the mid-80s in an effort to foster professional identity and visibility for the early childhood practitioner."

In these committee meetings no effort was made to review and synthesize research in defining the best practices. According to Johnson and McChesney Johnson (1992), this is how the guidelines for DAP were defined:

> DAP was never seen as needing to be exclusively or even primarily based on research literature. . . . Folklore and personal accounts of best practices passed on from one generation of teachers to the next counted a great deal. . . . The types of citations used to reference the NAEYC publications of DAP guidelines clearly indicate a reliance on sources other than articles reporting original empirical data (i.e., bona fide research). . . . Only 13 of 25 references cited in the DAP report were original reports of research. (Kontos 1989)

DAP was not based on bona fide research. Of the thirteen reports of bona fide research, only seven involved level-2 research. Four of the level-2 studies actually reported significant differences, and *none supported* DAP. Yet NAEYC published DAP guidelines for guiding legislative mandates and setting educational policy across America.

One reference of the thirteen (Goodlad and Anderson 1987) reviewed research on nongraded models but did not break these models down according to type of practice used (i.e., DAP or teacher-directed practices). Another source, Gutierrez and Slavin (1992), who did do such a breakdown, showed that the "nongraded organization can have a positive impact on student achievement if cross-age grouping is used to allow teachers to provide more direct instruction to students but not if it is used as a framework for individualized instruction" (p. 333). Gutierrez and Slavin also state:

> The movement toward developmentally appropriate early childhood education and its association with nongrading means that nongraded primary programs will probably be more integrated and thematic, and less academically structured or hierarchical [than the nongraded models evaluated in the research]. . . . Whether these instructional methods will have positive or negative effects on ultimate achievement is currently unknown. (1992, 370)

A superintendent in Oregon, where DAP was mandated through the Education Reform Act of 1992, sent me the following letter indicating that schools that were achieving at higher levels than the DAP pilot schools were asked to throw out their effective practices and adopt the less effective DAP:

> It never ceases to amaze me that no one seems to be actually utilizing the Oregon Statewide Assessment to ascertain program effectiveness and accountability. Over the past three years, in reviewing the listings of the Statewide Assessment scores by building and district throughout the state, it is very clear (and also disheartening) that many of the very schools which are touted as exemplary models do not have the test scores (measurable outcomes) to match.
>
> This is particularly discouraging for a school district such as ours, where we have . . . consistently achieved exemplary results in the Statewide Assessment; these proven successes are paid no heed. Given such examples, one cannot help but question the wisdom of our state's instructional "leaders."

In England, where DAP has been the officially endorsed approach for more than twenty years in the British infant and primary schools, achievement scores have gone steadily down. In 1992 the British Department of Education and Science published a scathing indictment of the DAP model (Department of Education and Science 1992).

In 1997, the NAEYC published a revision of the DAP guidelines (Brederkamp and Copple 1997). This revision does not reflect any major change from the original guidelines, nor do the guidelines reflect any conscientious reference to scientific research.

Whole Language

Several national organizations promote whole-language instruction as the official best practice for teaching language arts, including the NAEYC, the Whole Language Umbrella, the International Reading Association, and the National Council of Teachers of English. Whole-language instruction is similar to the language experience approach that characterized the TEEM model in Project Follow-Through. In the Follow-Through evaluation, the language experience approach (TEEM) had small positive effects in language arts performance but required so much time that the model had negative effects in mathematics.

Is there research to support whole-language instruction as an improved and effective practice? Whole-language advocates often claim that whole language is a philosophy, not a set of teaching activities, and, therefore, does not require evaluation. If the philosophy is expected to have any kind of effect on educational outcomes, however, then a scientific evaluation should determine if that effect occurs as expected. (See logs of E-mail discussions in October and November 1995, where whole-language leaders reject the use of comparative experimental studies to evaluate whole language: TAWL@listserv.arizona.edu.)

The evidence that whole-language instruction was a significant improvement over the language experience approach is weak. The fact that California claimed to adopt whole-language instruction in 1987 and then became the lowest-ranking state in the nation in fourth-grade reading seems to indicate that whole-language instruction is not much improved over the language experience approach and is certainly not the best practice in beginning reading instruction.

High/Scope

The emphasis of the High/Scope model is on play; academics are discouraged. (A preschool teacher in Illinois reported that she was told to stop posting the alphabet on the wall or risk losing the preschool's funding.) In Follow-Through, the model developed by the High/Scope Foundation (a cognitively oriented curriculum) resulted in much lower scores in mathematics (eleventh percentile) and language (twelfth percentile) than the usual performance level of children of poverty (around the twentieth percentile). On measures of self-esteem (affect) there were more negative outcomes for High/Scope than positive.

To support the adoption of the High/Scope model, advocates claim that, by emphasizing play and eliminating academics, children develop better self-esteem, which, over the long term, has more positive effects than an early academic focus. Most of the High/Scope research studies, however, compare the effects of a High/Scope preschool with those of no preschool at all. Only one study supports the distinctively nonacademic aspect of a High/Scope preschool. In that study of the Perry preschool program, fifty-four subjects were assigned to three preschool treatment groups (eighteen children to a group): a Direct Instruction academic approach, a High/Scope approach, and a common nursery school model. The children were followed through high school graduation. Along the way the performance of these groups was occasionally compared.

When the students were fifteen, Schweinhart, Weikart, and Larner (1986) reported that those who had received Direct Instruction in preschool reported higher rates of juvenile delinquency than the subjects who had been in High/Scope. On this self-report scale, students were asked questions such as, "Have you ever argued or fought with parents?" and indicated how many times they could recall doing this in their lifetime. Many critics of the study (Bereiter 1986a, 1986b; Gersten 1986; Gersten and Keating 1987; Gersten and White 1986) questioned the reliability of the self-report measure as an indicator of juvenile delinquency, first, because the objective data, such as actual arrests and suspensions from school, showed no differences between the groups. Second, some of the responses reported for the measure seemed unbelievable. For example, no group reported more than an average of two occasions (per student) on which they had ever argued or fought with their parents.

The High/Scope study is widely discussed at national conferences and in professional circles, and major policy decisions in America have been made on the basis of it. Decision makers, however, should look for more compelling evidence than that provided by one study, especially one conducted by the same organization that markets the product the study supports. (The High/Scope Foundation markets the High/Scope preschool model and conducted the study.)

In contrast to this one study of fifty-four subjects, Hirsch (1996) cites the results of decades of French data comparing the long-term effects of the academic preschool for three- and four-year-olds (*école maternelle*) with the nonacademic preschool (*crèche*):

> Recently, French social scientists completed longitudinal studies of some four thousand children on the long-term effects of *écoles maternelles* on the more than 30 percent of French *two*-year-olds who now attend these preschools. The results are striking. Those who attend school at a younger age are more effective academically and, by all indirect measures, better adjusted and happier for having had early exposure to challenging and stimulating early academic experiences.
>
> The French results are even more compelling from the standpoint of social justice. When disadvantaged children attend *écoles maternelles* at age two, their academic performance by grade six or seven equals that of highly advantaged children who have not attended preschool until age four. (p. 80)

Those findings contradict the conclusions of the High/Scope study. The French data are more compelling than the High/Scope study because (a) four thousand children were evaluated as opposed to only fifty-four in the High/Scope study, (b) the French researchers did not have a proprietary interest in the study, and (c) the High/Scope measures seemed technically unreliable.

Although the High/Scope study indicates that the effects of Direct Instruction do not hold over time, follow-up studies showed that the Direct Instruction Follow-Through children did benefit over the long term. Two studies (Darch, Gersten, and Taylor 1987; Meyer, Gersten, and Gutkin 1983) evaluated five cohorts of students (293 Direct Instruction students and 317 comparison students). Students using the Direct Instruction model through grade 3 showed higher graduation rates, lower dropout rates, more promotions to the next grade, more applications to college, and more acceptances to college. All these differences were statistically significant. For example, 60 percent of the Direct Instruction students graduated from high school compared with 40 percent in the comparison group.

Some have pointed out that, though the children in the Direct Instruction model generally caught up with their middle-class peers by the end of third grade, they lost ground again in grades 4–12. A 60 percent graduation rate, for example, is far from ideal. Perhaps if the Follow-Through children had attended the same schools their middle-class peers attended during the later years, one could expect them to have maintained their gains. The quality of their education after grade 3, however, was not the same as that of middle-class children. Gersten describes his observations while gathering the follow-up data:

> I spent six months . . . riding the subway lines to every vocational high school in Brooklyn and driving through swampy country roads in South Carolina to isolated high schools. It was impossible not to see how segregated education is or to ignore consistently low teacher expectations, as well as the apathy, sarcasm, and latent hostility present in some of the high schools. (Gersten and Keating 1987, 31)

Nevertheless, the evidence from these follow-up studies indicated that children of poverty receiving Direct Instruction in grades K–3 maintained a lasting advantage.

National Committees

Rather than use research to develop ideas, many national interest groups such as the NAEYC are convening committees, which might be a good idea if the committees were dedicated to synthesizing research, but the reports from these committees often indicate that this is not their intent. In fact, their teaching recommendations often contradict research and reject a scientific model for building a knowledge base; that is, they reject level-2 and level-3 research.

The National Council of Teachers of Mathematics (NCTM), using a similar committee approach to define teaching practice, convened a committee to establish NCTM standards. As standards for what students should know and be able to do, those standards are not a problem; however, the NCTM did not translate these standards into assessments of students' learning but into vignettes to illustrate the teaching practices that teachers should use.

As standards for telling teachers how to teach, the NCTM standards are not research based but rather represent the consensus of opinions of the people on the NCTM committee. The NCTM standards document itself describes the recommendations as a "research agenda," not a research synthesis. One member of the committee suggested that the NCTM set up a pilot school to demonstrate that the NCTM teaching recommendations would result in the achievement of the NCTM standards. That this suggestion is mentioned in the document is the committee's acknowledgment that no level-3 research exists to support the teaching practices it recommends.

A parent wrote to the NCTM requesting data to support the adoption of the teaching practices recommended in the NCTM standards. The NCTM's reply indicated that there were no such data: "First, this reply is to inform you that I am not aware of any research study that relates the 'adoption' of the NCTM's Standards to improved scores on the Iowa Tests of Basic Skills, a fact that your school district's administrators and board of trustees have correctly stated." The NCTM letter points out that the content of the standards "transcend reliance on paper and pencil tests to assess students' aptitudes and achievement in mathematics." Data to support the teaching recommendations do not exist because the kinds of measures the NCTM needs to evaluate the learning it desires have not been developed.

If no assessment tools exist for adequately evaluating the NCTM standards for student learning, how was it possible to develop a research base for the teaching standards that were published in 1991? Why were the assessment standards not developed first, instead of much later, in 1995? Without ways to evaluate the learning that the NCTM recommends, it is impossible to use research to identify the teaching practices that best accomplish those learning goals.

Despite the hypothetical nature of its teaching recommendations, the NCTM engaged in a widespread national marketing campaign to promote them. Now that the NCTM has convinced most of the education world that the best way to teach is its way, the research journal published by the NCTM does not seem interested in evaluating questions regarding the best teaching practices. My colleagues have submitted many level-2 research studies to the *Journal of Research in Mathematics Education* (*JRME*) since the publication of the NCTM standards. These studies have all been rejected. Although it may have been that they were all of unpublishable quality, it seems more than coincidence that almost no level-2 research has been published in the *JRME* and that the rejected studies' conclusions were inconsistent with the recommendations of the NCTM committee. In one rejection letter, the editor actually acknowledged that the study was rejected because the findings of the study were not consistent with the opinion of the NCTM committee.

The Research Advisory Committee for the *JRME* openly recommended in 1995, as a matter of policy, that the journal not publish level-2 research. It recommended instead that the journal publish "disciplined inquiry," apparently something different from scientific inquiry: "Disciplined inquiry is as much an orientation as an accomplishment" (Research Advisory Council of the National Council of Teachers of Mathematics 1995, 301). One can publish one's "orientation" in *JRME,* but comparative studies identifying the features of a superior curriculum are not acceptable: "The question 'Is Curriculum A better than Curriculum B?' is not a good research question because it is not really answerable." If this question is not answerable, then the NCTM committee has no business making recommendations regarding curriculum design and teaching practice.

We often hear about the inadequacy of the scientific paradigm. The premise for this argument holds that humans are so unique and complex that the effects of any teaching procedure on learning either cannot be measured or will be unpredictable. If there is no expectation that a specific teaching practice will work with more than the sample with which it was tested, then there is no basis for recommending the practice. If there are recommendations to teachers, scientific research should support them. Those who reject the scientific paradigm cannot possibly make recommendations to teachers. To make a teaching recommendation to someone else is to step into a scientific paradigm. Science clearly stands in the way of faddism.

Conclusion

Scientific research does not guide the development of the professional knowledge base of teaching. As Hirsch (1996) points out, the recommendations of national interest groups such as the National Council of Teachers of English, the National Council of Teachers of Mathematics, the National Association for the Education of Young Children, and many more highly influential organizations in education are better characterized as "worst practice" than as "best practice." The teaching practices taught in colleges of education are generally no different. By ignoring scientific research and promoting prejudices, the professional support system for education often serves as an obstacle rather than as a resource in disseminating the knowledge that is crucial to the success of public education.

Most likely, privatizing education would not solve this problem, for it would change the decision makers without necessarily changing the way in which decisions are made. Selecting instructional approaches based on the personal prejudices of local leaders is just as unscientific as selecting them based on the personal prejudices of national leaders. Furthermore, those national interest groups whose influence in education is at the root of the problem are not publicly funded. They would continue to exist in a system of private education, even after public education ceased to exist, and they would probably remain at least as influential as they are now. If history is an example, private schools generally implemented whole language and developmentally appropriate practices with as much vigor as the public schools.

Privatizing the education system without changing the way the professional knowledge base is built would be similar to allowing the medical profession to operate without the safeguards of the Food and Drug Administration. Consumers would not be able to discriminate quacks from doctors' practicing sound medicine. Ensuring that scientific research supports new procedures entering the professional canon for teachers, and ensuring that this knowledge is disseminated in reliable ways through university teacher training and school-based staff development programs, requires a coordinated national effort. American education will not be able to produce what it is capable of producing until the professional support system for education is fixed.

References

Adams, G., and S. Engelmann (1996). *Research on Direct Instruction: 20 Years beyond DISTAR*. Seattle, Wash.: Educational Achievement Systems.

Bereiter, C. (1986a). "Does Direct Instruction Cause Delinquency?" *Early Childhood Research Quarterly* 1: 289–92.

Bereiter, C. (1986b). "'Mountains of Evidence,' Said to Contradict Study on Effects of Preschool." *Education Week* 5, no. 57: 19.

Bereiter, C., and M. Kurland (1981). "A Constructive Look at Follow Through Results." *Interchange* 12: 1–22.

Bock, G., L. Stebbins, and E. Proper (1977). *Education as Experimentation: A Planned Variation Model*. Volume IV-B. Cambridge, Mass.: Abt Associates.

Brandt, R. (1986). "On Long-Term Effects of Early Education: A Conversation with Lawrence Schweinhart." *Educational Leadership* 44: 14–18.

Brederkamp, S., and C. Copple (eds.) (1997). *Developmentally Appropriate Practice in Early Childhood Programs*. Revised edition. Washington, D.C.: National Association for the Education of Young Children.

Center, Y., K. Wheldall, L. Freeman, L. Outhred, and M. McNaught (1995). "An Experimental Evaluation of Reading Recovery." *Reading Research Quarterly* 30: 240–63.

Darch, C., R. Gersten, and R. Taylor (1987). "Evaluation of Williamsburg County Direct Instruction Program: Factors Leading to Success in Rural Elementary Programs." *Research in Rural Education* 4: 111–18.

DeFord, D. E., R. Estice, M. Fried, C. E. Lyons, and G. S. Pinnell (1993). *The Reading Recovery Program: Executive Summary 1984–92*. Columbus: Ohio State University.

Department of Education and Science (London) (1992). *Curriculum Organization and Classroom Practice in Primary Schools: A Discussion Paper*. London: Department of Education and Science.

Ellis, A., and J. Fouts (1993). *Research on Educational Innovations*. Princeton, N.J.: Eye on Education.

Ellis, A., and J. Fouts (1994). *Research on School Restructuring*. Princeton, N.J.: Eye on Education.

Gersten, R. (1986). "Response to 'Consequences of Three Preschool Curriculum Models through Age 15.'" *Early Childhood Research Quarterly* 1: 293–302.

Gersten, R., and T. Keating (1987). "Long-Term Benefits from Direct Instruction." *Educational Leadership*: 28–31.

Gersten, R., and W.A.T. White (1986). "Castles in the Sand: Response to Schweinhart and Weikart." *Educational Leadership* 44: 19–20.

Glass, G. V., and G. Camilli (1981). *"FT" Evaluation.* Washington, D.C.: National Institute of Education.

Glynn, T., T. Crooks, N. Bethune, K. Ballard, and J. Smith (1989). "Reading Recovery in Context: Implementation and Outcome." *Educational Psychology* 12, nos. 3–4: 249–61.

Graham, S. (1984). "Teacher Feelings and Student Thought: An Attributional Approach to Affect in the Classroom." *Elementary School Journal* 85: 91–104.

Gutierrez, R., and R. Slavin (1992). "Achievement Effects of the Nongraded Elementary School: Summary of a Best Evidence Synthesis." *Review of Educational Research* 62, no. 4: 333–76.

Hiebert, E. (1994). "Reading Recovery in the United States: What Difference Does It Make to an Age Cohort?" *Educational Researcher* 23, no. 9: 15–25.

Hirsch, E. D. (1996). *The Schools We Need and Why We Don't Have Them.* New York: Doubleday.

House, E., G. Glass, L. McLean, and D. Walker (1978). "No Simple Answer: Critique of FT Evaluation." *Harvard Educational Review* 48, no. 2: 128–60.

Iverson, S., and W. E. Tunmer (1993). "Phonological Processing Skills and the Reading Recovery Program." *Journal of Educational Psychology* 85, no. 1: 112–26.

Johnson, J., and K. McChesney Johnson (1992). "Clarifying the Developmental Perspective in Response to Carta, Schwartz, Atwater, and McConnell." *Topics in Early Childhood Special Education* 12, no. 4: 439–57.

Kameenui, E., and D. Carnine (eds.) (in press). *Educational Tools for Diverse Learners.* Merrill.

Kennedy, M. (1978). "Findings from the Follow-Through Planned Variation Study." *Educational Researcher* (June): 3–11.

Kontos, S. (1989). *Developmentally Appropriate Practice: What Does Re-*

search Tell Us? Indianapolis: Indiana Association for the Education of Young Children.

Lawton, M. (1996). "Support for Private School Vouchers Is on the Increase Gallup Poll Reports." *Education Week* 16, no. 1: 18–19.

Lindsley, O. (1992). "Why Aren't Effective Teaching Tools Widely Adopted?" *Journal of Applied Behavior Analysis* 25, nos. 1–2.

McDaniels, G. (1975). "Evaluation of Follow-Through." *Educational Researcher* 4: 7–11.

Meyer, L., R. Gersten, and J. Gutkin (1983). "Direct Instruction: A Project Follow Through Success Story in an Inner-City School." *Elementary School Journal* 84: 241–52.

Pinnell, G. S., C. A. Lyons, D. E. DeFord, A. S. Bryk, and M. Seltzer (1994). "Comparing Instructional Models for the Literacy Education of High-Risk First Graders." *Reading Research Quarterly* 29, no. 1: 9–38.

Research Advisory Council of the National Council of Teachers of Mathematics (1995). "Research and Practice." *Journal for Research in Mathematics Education* 26, no. 4: 300–303.

Schweinhart, L., and D. Weikart (1986). "Schweinhart and Weikart Reply." *Educational Leadership* 44: 22.

Schweinhart, L., and D. Weikart (1988). "Education for Young Children Living in Poverty: Child-Initiated or Teacher-Directed Instruction?" *Elementary School Journal* 89: 213–25.

Schweinhart, L., D. Weikart, and M. Larner (1986). "Consequences of Three Preschool Curriculum Models through Age 15." *Early Childhood Research Quarterly* 1: 15–45.

Shanahan, T., and R. Barr (1995). "Reading Recovery: An Independent Evaluation of the Effects of an Early Instructional Intervention for At-Risk Learners." *Reading Research Quarterly* 30, no. 4: 958–96.

Shanker, A. (May 12, 1996). "Where We Stand: Lots of Bull but No Beef." Http://www.aft.org/.

Stanovich, K. (1994). "Romance versus Reality." *Reading Teacher* 47, no. 4: 280–91.

Stebbins, L., R. St. Pierre, E. Proper, R. Anderson, and T. Cerva (1977). *Education as Experimentation: A Planned Variation Model.* Volume IV-A. Cambridge, Mass.: Abt Associates.

Stigler, J. W., and H. Stevenson (1991). "How Asian Teachers Polish Each Lesson to Perfection." *American Educator* (spring): 12–47.

Watkins, C. (1996). "Follow Through: Why Didn't We?" *Effective School Practices* 15, no. 1: 57–66

Weikart, D., A. Epstein, L. Schweinhart, and J. Bond (1978). *The Ypsilanti Preschool Curriculum Demonstration Project: Preschool Years and Longitudinal Results.* Ypsilanti, Mich.: High/Scope.

Jack M. Fletcher and G. Reid Lyon

Reading:
A Research-Based Approach

In recent years, considerable national attention has been focused on the reading skills of children in the United States. Some argue that reading failure rates are increasing; others respond that the concerns about reading levels in children are manufactured. Despite this controversy, the performance of children on measures of reading proficiency has been of sufficient concern to result in highly publicized state-level reading initiatives in California and Texas, a presidential initiative to enhance children's reading skills, and considerable scrutiny of reading in many areas of the country.

In this context a body of research has evolved on how children learn to read and why some fail (see Appendix). This research, sponsored at the federal level by the National Institute of Child Health and Human Development (NICHD), has existed for more than thirty years (Lyon 1995; Lyon, Alexander, and Yaffe 1997). It is not the only existing research on the development of reading skills and reading failure, but it does represent a comprehensive research program that has attracted attention

Supported in part by NICHD grants R01 HD30855, R01 HD28712, P01 HD21888, and P50 HD25802. We thank Benita Blachman, David Denton, Rebecca Felton, Barbara Foorman, Richard Olson, Joseph Torgesen, and Frank Vellutino for their helpful comments and Rita Taylor for manuscript preparation.

because of nationwide concern about children's ability to read. Perhaps the best indication of the interest in this research comes from a recent report to Congress, wherein the director of the NICHD, Dr. Duane Alexander, emphasized three major areas of progress: The first was research on reducing the incidence of sudden infant death syndrome by modifying infant sleep positions. The second was laboratory research on the role of folate acid metabolism in causing spina bifida and other neural tube defects, which led to legislation requiring the addition of Vitamin B to bread. The third area was the NICHD research on reading and reading failure. Unfortunately, the NICHD research has not yet significantly affected how children are taught to read in school, so that a gap continues to exist between what we know about reading and how children are taught to read. As Benita Blachman, a well-known reading researcher, stated in testimony in Washington:

> The good news is that there have been scientific breakthroughs in our knowledge about the development of literacy. We know a great deal about how to address reading problems even before they begin. . . . The tragedy is that we are not exploiting what is known about reducing the incidence of reading failure. Specifically, the instruction currently being provided to our children does not reflect what we know from research. Direct, systematic instruction about the alphabetic code is not routinely provided in kindergarten and first grade, despite the fact that, given what we know at the moment, this might be the most powerful weapon in the fight against illiteracy. (Blachman 1996, 66–67)

The NICHD research supports a prominent role for explicit instruction in phonics and phonological awareness skills (i.e., alphabetic principle) for beginning reading instruction, particularly for children at risk for reading failure. It also shows how these skills are involved in learning to read for all children, regardless of how they are taught. The NICHD intervention research, however, is sometimes equated with either an exclusive phonics approach or research addressing only children with reading problems.

Both interpretations are inaccurate. The intervention studies are consistent with the larger body of research in showing that explicitly teaching phonics and phonological awareness skills is an important part of early reading instruction. Gains in early reading skills are mediated by the effect of the intervention on phonological processing abilities. The interventions used in the NICHD studies, however, involve more than explicit teaching of phonics. They also include a major emphasis on reading and writing in environments that include good literature, reading for enjoyment, and other practices believed to facilitate the development of reading skills and literacy (Adams 1990). Hence, the NICHD studies are consistent with educational research highlighting the importance of *balanced* approaches to reading instruction (Adams, Treiman, and Pressley 1997). Moreover, these studies are based on a large body of NICHD research on how children learn to read. The intervention studies apply the findings of this research. If the NICHD had never funded a single study of intervention or learning disabilities, this research on normal processes of reading development would still have major policy implications for teaching children to read.

In the remainder of this chapter, we outline some of the major findings of this research, which is now taking place in thirty-six sites in North America. The research that focuses on reading failure was based on earlier ongoing research—also funded in part by NICHD—that critically analyzed the nature of reading skills, how children learn to read, and the bases of reading failure (Lyon et al. 1997). In fact, the NICHD funds research on learning processes at all levels—cellular, experiential, neurological and in humans and animals. The NICHD also funds research on many aspects of the reading process, such as eye movements in beginning and skilled readers, relationships of language and reading in nonimpaired children and adults, social and biological factors in literacy, and other areas that affect reading but do not involve disability.

During the past thirty-three years, NICHD reading scientists have studied, at thirty-six research sites, the reading development of 34,501 children and adults, including 21,860 skilled readers and 12,641 impaired readers. As the titles of the selected research projects in the appendix indicate, approximately 50 percent of the current NICHD research effort in reading is devoted to research on how language, reading, and reading-related skills emerge in proficient readers; the other 50 percent addresses factors that impede the acquisition of those skills. As the titles of the research projects in the appendix indicate, multiple processes related to reading—phonological awareness, word recognition, reading fluency and automaticity, reading comprehension processes, and social and biological factors in literacy—are currently being addressed by the NICHD-sponsored research. There is also considerable research on reading and reading failure not funded by the NICHD, but our report focuses on findings obtained from NICHD research.

Prevalence and Outcomes

One set of issues addressed by NICHD research involves the number of children with reading problems and the long-term course of reading difficulties, which led Congress in 1985 to authorize NICHD to expand its research program on reading and disabilities in reading and learning. The magnitude of the reading problem is significant. From NICHD and non-NICHD research, we know that at least 10 million school-age children in the United States are poor readers. Reading problems occur with equal frequency in boys and girls; in schools, however, boys are identified as learning disabled in reading four times more often than girls, largely on the basis of behavioral characteristics that lead to referral of the child for special education (Shaywitz et al. 1990). The prevalence of reading disability is approximately 20 percent of school-age children depending on how disability is defined and where it is studied (Shaywitz et al. 1992). It may be higher than in previous epidemiological studies in the 1970s (Benton and Pearl 1978), but variations in definition and the absence of comparable assessments over the past twenty years make that difficult to establish (Lyon 1995; Lyon et al. 1997). Whether rates of reading failure are increasing or decreasing begs the question of the significance of reading failure rates. The number of children who are identified as disabled or who do not meet basic levels of proficiency on reading assessments such as the National Assessment of Reading Proficiency (more than 40 percent in 1994) should be cause for alarm regardless of whether the rate is changing.

Long-term outcomes of early reading difficulties are poor. In one recent study, 74 percent of children who were poor readers in the third grade remained poor readers in the ninth grade. Figure 1, which displays growth in reading skills in a large group of children studied from kindergarten through ninth grade, indicates that most poor readers never catch up on their reading skills (Francis et al. 1996). This pattern is apparent even before the third grade. In another study, Juel (1988) found that word recognition skills at the end of the first grade were strongly related to reading proficiency at the end of the fourth grade. Indeed, almost nine of ten children who were deficient in reading in the first grade were poor readers in the fourth grade. Similarly, Torgesen et al. (1997) reported that more than eight of ten children with severe word reading problems at the end of the first grade performed below the average range at the beginning of the third grade. Hence, it is not surprising that special education

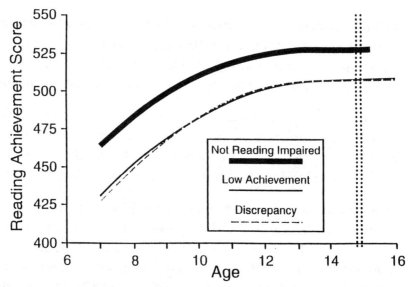

Figure 1.   Growth in reading skills from grade 1 through grade 9 for children identified as *not reading impaired* and *as disabled in reading* (discrepant with IQ score or low achieving) in grade 3. Regardless of definition, most children who are impaired in reading do not catch up in their reading skills (Francis et al. 1996). Reprinted with permission of the American Psychological Association.

figures from the U.S. Department of Education (Office of Special Education Programs 1993) show that less than 25 percent of children in special education were identified as learning disabled before 1980. In figure 2 we see the number of children identified for different eligibility categories in special education from 1977 to 1993. By 1993 more than 50 percent of eligible children were in the learning disabled category. Many factors underlie this increase (Allington 1991), but instruction should be considered. Of particular interest is the report that, of all children identified as learning disabled by public schools, 70–80 percent are primarily impaired in reading; 90 percent of those children have difficulties with word recognition skills (Lerner 1989). Critical questions are how word recognition skills are learned, and why poor readers have difficulty with single-word skills. The answers to these

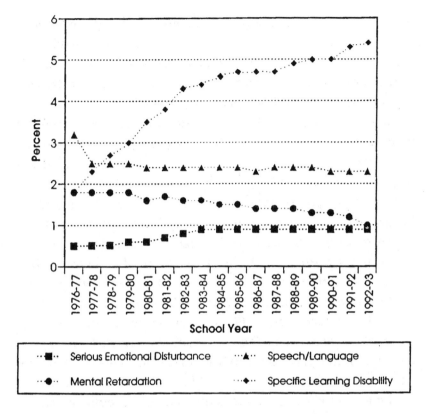

Figure 2.   Percentage of children identified in the most common educational eligibility categories from 1977 to 1993 (Office of Special Education Programs, U.S. Department of Education, 1993).

questions reside in research on the relationship of language and reading.

Language and Reading

What we know about reading and language begins with a simple observation made by the noted speech scientist Alvin M. Liberman, who has long argued that reading is dependent on language but is not a natural outgrowth of language. As Liberman (1997, 4–5) recently observed:

> A proper theory of speech is essential to an understanding of how people read—the most relevant consideration arises out of the deep biological gulf that separates the two processes. Speech, on the one side, is a product of biological evolution, standing as the most obvious, and arguably the most important, of our species-typical behaviors. Reading/writing, on the other, did not evolve biologically, but rather developed (in some cultures) as a secondary response to that which evolution had already produced. A consequence is that we are biologically destined to speak, not to read or write. Accordingly, we are all good at speech, but disabled as readers and writers; the difference among us in reading/writing is simply that some are fairly easy to cure and some are not.

In other words, oral language, which humans have possessed for millions of years, usually unfolds as a natural biological progression. It is not an automatic unfolding, however, as is commonly believed. Environmental factors also have significant influences on early language development. The difference is that most children develop language proficiency through interactions that are not explicitly intended to teach the child to talk. In contrast, written language is an artificial construction built on oral language. Thus, reading, which humans have possessed for only about four thousand years, does not reflect a biological process that emerges naturally. Although children vary in how explicitly reading must be taught, even children who seem to learn to read at an early age have a period in which the nature of print and its relationship to language is brought explicitly to their attention (Gough and Hillinger 1980; A. M. Liberman 1997). Given that reading must be taught—how else would we explain illiteracy in literate cultures?—the questions that NICHD and other researchers have puzzled over are, What aspects of reading must be taught? Why do children fail to learn to read? and How do you best teach poor readers to read?

What Must Be Taught

The critical component of reading that must be taught is the relationship of print to speech. Many other components of reading, particularly those that relate to comprehension, are outgrowths of the child's facility for language. For example, in what is described as the "simple view" of reading, Gough and Tumner (1986) proposed that reading consists of two primary components: *decoding*, or word recognition, and language *comprehension*, both of which are necessary for reading proficiency. Children do not become proficient readers unless both components are fully developed. In other words, children who cannot decipher the words on a page in a fluent and accurate manner will struggle to comprehend the meaning of the text; without proficient language comprehension skills, even children who recognize the words may not necessarily understand their meaning. Word recognition skills are intrinsic to reading, reflecting the need to decipher print, whereas language comprehension pervades all areas of literacy. Reading comprehension skills can (and should) be taught (Adams et al. 1997), but word recognition skills are essential for the child to become proficient. Hence, in the simple view, reading proficiency is the product of word recognition and language comprehension skills; some of the controversy among reading professionals is not whether both sets of skills must be mastered but how children master these skills and how explicitly these skills must be taught. The broader underlying issues involve philosophical views on learning and development, such as whether children master skills or construct knowledge. The NICHD research clearly stems from a skills perspective.

Research supported by the NICHD shows that learning to read is a developmental process children go through in acquiring proficiency. Because proficient readers employ processes that are different from beginning readers, research on good readers may not fully apply to beginning readers. Skilled readers do not gloss or skip over words when reading text; they sample nearly every word. Phonological codes that involve the sounds of words and help the reader decipher the words are activated early in word recognition in beginning and skilled readers (Rayner, Sereono, Lesch, and Pollatsek 1995). However, the task for the beginning reader is to move from the early phases of "sounding out" words to the more skilled phase in which word recognition occurs almost instaneously. This developmental change allows the word recognition process to occur fluently, automatically, and rapidly enough to allow for the abstraction of meaning from text. Without efficient (automatic) word recognition skills, comprehension is impaired even when the underlying comprehension processes are well developed.

How do children learn word recognition skills (i.e., decode)? The answers have their origins in research from the NICHD-supported Haskins Laboratories in New Haven, Connecticut, that extends over a thirty-year period (see Brady and Shankweiler 1991; A. M. Liberman 1996; Lyon et al. 1997). In the late 1960s and early 1970s, investigators at the Haskins Laboratories were studying the relationship of speech and language. Through a series of experiments, they discovered that how speech is articulated influences the relationship between spoken and written language (A. M. Liberman 1996). This relationship involves how the sound structures of language are represented in speech (i.e., phonology). Speech can be broken down into sounds smaller than the word or the syllable called *phonemes*, the smallest parts of speech that make a difference in the meaning of a word. A critical discovery was that phonemes overlap, or are *coarticulated*, in the speech stream (Liberman, Cooper, Shankweiler, and Studdert-Kennedy 1967). As Blachman (1997) reports, the late Isabelle Y. Liberman and her colleagues (I. Y. Liberman 1971, 1973) expanded this discovery to the processing of speech, observing that a fundamental task for the beginning reader is understanding not only that speech can be broken down into phonemic segments but that these segments are represented by the alphabet in printed form. Liberman and her colleagues undertook a series of studies of how children learn to read, showing that beginning readers must become aware of the phonological structure of oral language (i.e., phonological awareness) in order to appreciate how print represents speech (Brady and Shankweiler 1991; A. M. Liberman 1996; I. Y. Liberman et al. 1989). Developing this awareness, however, is not automatic because phonemes are not separated in producing speech, which makes the phonetic structure of speech obscure. Yet being aware of how print represents the phonological structure of spoken words is the key skill specific to reading that children must learn. That awareness is the basis for scaffolding written language onto oral language.

The early (and continuing) work of investigators at the Haskins Laboratories—the cornerstone of the research supported by NICHD on reading failure—has had international influence leading to a large accumulation of data supporting the key role of phonological awareness. That research also led to non-NICHD-supported longitudinal studies of preschoolers in Great Britain and Sweden showing that early activities involving phonological awareness skills (i.e., rhyming and alliteration games) helped reading skills later in school relative to the reading skills of children who did not receive these activities (Bradley and Bryant 1983; Lundberg, Frost, and Peterson 1988). Other NICHD and non-NICHD studies of children who varied in reading levels, socioeconomic backgrounds, and literacy experiences have also shown that explicit training in phonological awareness skills before first grade is associated with better reading skills later (Byrne and Fielding-Barnesly 1995; Torgesen 1997).

Phonological awareness is only one, albeit large, component of learning to read. Many processes and experiences are critical for the development of beginning reading skills (Adams 1990; Adams et al. in press; Share and Stanovich 1995). These include not only phonological awareness skills but also letter and print awareness, early language experiences, and a literacy background. As Adams (1990) pointed out, however, these early processes are only a means to ends, with one goal being efficient word recognition. In addition, as Gough and Tumner (1986) noted, the second goal, comprehension, depends not only on word recognition skills but also on the child's general capacities for language comprehension, as well as other cognitive processes involved in processing text, such as short-term memory. These processes can be fostered through effective teaching of strategies and can be understood as the construction of meaning, representing an active process in which the reader, teacher, and text interact (Brown, Pressley, Van Meter, and Schuder 1996). Text reading processes, however, do not explain why most children fail to learn to read. In the next section we review NICHD research on reading failure, for it is with poor readers that the importance of word recognition processes and phonological awareness skills are most apparent.

Why Children Fail to Read

Word Recognition Deficits

Fundamental to this question of reading failure is a set of observations that make it possible to approach poor reading scientifically. Although we know that reading problems occur primarily at the level of the single word and involve the ability to decode printed words (Shaywitz 1996; Torgesen 1997; Vellutino 1979, 1991), the basis of this problem was not clearly established until more recently. Research on developing reading skills in nondisabled children, and word recognition skills in poor readers, established that word recognition problems arise from problems breaking apart words and syllables into phonemes. This relationship is apparent in the majority of poor readers, including children, adolescents, and adults at all levels of IQ, and in children and adults from linguistically and culturally diverse backgrounds. To reiterate, reading is *alphabetic*, which means that, for languages such as English and Spanish, the code is in the alphabet. Even in languages that are not alphabetic, like Chinese, the code is still based on phonology and relationships of phonemes to the characters (logograms) of Chinese writing.

Simply put, word recognition, or decoding, is looking at a word and cracking a code. The code is in the print but is essentially an alphabetic one whereby the child must learn to relate phonological structures in spoken words to print. Thus, proficient readers can come close to pronouncing words never before heard, much less seen, and can even pronounce pseudowords (i.e., nonsense words) with a phonetic structure, such as *crad*. Hence, when children develop word recognition skills they become aware that words have an internal structure based on their sounds and represented by the alphabet. Comprehension of the word thus becomes almost instantaneous.

When children learn how print represents the internal structure of words, they become accurate at word recognition; when they learn to recognize words quickly and automatically, they become fluent. Many children seem to figure out these relationships regardless of how they are taught. For some children—the actual percentage is difficult to estimate, but it is probably at least

20 percent and most likely more—this relationship is not straightforward and may need to be explicitly taught; hence the problem we have today.

Causes of Poor Reading

The NICHD research has *not* found the processes underlying reading disability to be *qualitatively* different from those processes associated with early reading proficiency. Reading problems occur as part of a natural, unbroken continuum of ability. What causes good reading also leads to poor reading when the processes are deficient (Shaywitz et al. 1992). Many factors underlie the cognitive deficiencies associated with reading failure. Although these causes are multiple, most children's problems occur at the level of the single word. The NICHD has evaluated the following factors:

Neurological.   Brain activity when reading for the sounds of words, such as whether they rhyme, is different in good and poor readers (see Lyon and Rumsey 1997). Specific areas of the brain are involved, but a distinct neural signature has not yet been defined. Research on brain structure in poor readers shows subtle variations that are not consistent across studies. Much of this research has been done with adults who have a history of reading problems. Needed studies of young readers are under way. Recent studies using new technologies for measuring brain functions are promising but only beginning to emerge (Shaywitz 1996). A key question is whether improved reading may actually result in changes in brain functions.

Familial.   Reading problems run in families and cut across all sociocultural groups. These problems can have a genetic component, but several different genes are involved (Cardon et al. 1994; Grigorenko et al. 1997). In addition, genetic factors account for only about half of the variability in reading skills, which means that the environment has a significant influence on reading outcomes. For example, adults who read poorly may be less likely to read to their children. The quality of reading instruction may be more critical for children when there is a family history of poor reading.

Cultural and Linguistic Diversity. Both NICHD and non-NICHD studies show that print exposure, levels of parental literacy, and reading to the child are important (Adams 1990). Recent research, however, suggests that these influences are somewhat overestimated because intervention studies have been successful in culturally and linguistically diverse populations where home literacy experiences are often limited (Foorman et al. 1997a, 1997b, 1998; Torgesen 1997).

Instructional. The influence of instruction in reading has been underestimated, as we will see when we turn to intervention studies. What is important is that the skills that prevent poor reading must be taught early—in kindergarten, grade 1, and grade 2. For many children, these skills may need to be taught explicitly over several years.

Teaching Poor Readers to Read

The NICHD has supported several studies of how to prevent reading failure and how to intervene with poor readers. These studies have been coordinated by centers at Bowman-Gray Medical School, Florida State University, the State University of New York at Albany, the University of Colorado, and the University of Texas-Houston Health Science Center. The studies have taken place in multiple settings and include children with identified reading problems (Felton 1993; Torgesen 1997; Wise and Olsen 1995), children served in Title I programs (Foorman et al. 1998), kindergarten children at risk for reading failure (Foorman et al. 1997a; Torgesen 1997), and children reading poorly in populations that are predominantly middle class with relatively good literacy experiences (Scanlon and Vellutino 1996; Vellutino et al. 1996). In addition, more-recent NICHD-supported investigations have been initiated at Georgia State University, Tufts University, Syracuse University, the Hospital for Sick Children in Toronto, and the University of Washington.

The primary goals of the intervention studies have been to (1) identify the conditions, abilities, and processes that must be available for a child to develop robust word recognition and reading comprehension skills and (2) identify for which children with reading difficulties are different instructional factors and components most beneficial and at which stages of reading development (Lyon and Moats 1997). With these goals in mind, these studies share common features, including the assessment methodologies. The studies are based on research (described above) showing how normal children learn to read and applying this research to the study of reading failure. Hence, the studies share an emphasis on the effectiveness of teaching word recognition skills, usually through phonics or phonological awareness training or both. In many studies, the research was designed to evaluate the degree of explicitness required to teach word recognition skills. Instruction in word recognition skills, however, occurs along with opportunities for applications to reading and writing, exposure to literature, and other practices believed to facilitate the development of reading skills in proficient readers. This reflects one of the oldest observations of any form of teaching or training—a targeted skill cannot be learned without opportunities for practice and application. Because of the interest in these studies, each NICHD site will be discussed separately.

The Bowman-Gray Reading Intervention Studies

Brown and Felton (1990) and Felton (1993) compared the efficacy of interventions defined as *code-based*, which emphasized identification of words based on letter-sound associations and patterns, and *meaning-based*, which emphasized identification of words based on context supplemented by partial letter-sound cues (i.e., beginning and ending sounds). The children were identified at the end of kindergarten as at risk for reading failure based either on deficient phonological awareness skills from tests administered by the researchers or by teacher identification or both. In addition, children were also followed who received the school's standard instructional program. Thus, kindergarten children were randomly assigned to one of two reading instruction programs for first and second grade, along with a third group who received the school's standard curriculum. Children were taught in small groups in regular classrooms within the child's home school.

The meaning-based approach used a basal reading program, whereas the code-based approach explicitly taught phonics. These programs were selected because they taught similar word recognition skills in the first- and second-grade curriculums but varied as to whether the instruction in word recognition skills was explicitly presented by the teacher. At the end of the second grade children who had received the code-based instruction earned significantly higher mean scores than children who had received the meaning-based approach on measures of word recognition and spelling. Felton (1993) concluded that five elements were critical to a beginning program for children at risk of reading failure: (1) direct instruction in language analysis; (2) explicit teaching of the alphabetic code; (3) reading and spelling must be taught simultaneously; (4) reading instruction must be sufficiently intense for learning to occur; and (5) using decodable words and texts enhanced automaticity.

The Florida State University Reading Intervention Studies

Torgesen et al. (1997) identified 180 children in kindergarten who were at the bottom twelfth percentile in phonological processing skills. Those children, who varied widely in their general verbal ability and home literacy environments, were randomly assigned to four instructional conditions, two of which were experimental and two of which were control conditions. The most important way the two experimental instructional programs differed from each other was in the amount and explicitness of instruction in phonological awareness and phonemic reading strategies. In the explicit approach, phonological awareness was taught by helping children discover the articulatory positions and mouth movements associated with each of the phonemes in English (Lindamood and Lindamood 1975). These children also received extensive practice in applying phonemic decoding strategies to individual words. In the other approach, phonological awareness was stimulated during writing activities, and children were taught letter-sound correspondences as they learned new sight words. A much higher proportion of time was devoted to reading and writing meaningful text. In both conditions, children began reading and discussing connected, meaningful text as soon as they could read just a few words. That component is critical because children who are poor readers tend to spend less time actually reading and writing (Allington 1991; Juel 1988), yet more time on these activities is critical for skill mastery.

The children in each instructional condition received eighty minutes of individualized (one to one) supplemental instruction each week over a two-and-a-half year period beginning in mid-kindergarten. Half the instructional sessions for each child were led by well-trained teachers, and half were led by instructional aides. The children also received regular classroom instruction, which varied widely depending on whether teachers viewed the instructional program as emphasizing phonics or as more context or literature based.

The results indicated that, at the end of the second grade, children who received explicit instruction in the alphabetic principle had much stronger reading skills than children in all the other groups. In addition, children who received the most explicit instruction showed the lowest need to be held back a grade (9 percent), with hold-back rates in the other three conditions ranging from 25 percent (implicit phonics) to 30 percent (classroom support condition) to 41 percent (no-treatment comparison group). As a group, children in the explicit condition demonstrated word-level reading skills that were in the middle of the average range. In this same group, however, 24 percent of the children were still well below average. Extrapolated to the entire population, this would lead to an overall failure rate of 2.4 percent. This figure, of course, is far below the 20 percent reported for children with reading disabilities (based on word recognition definitions) reported above. Other analyses showed that growth in reading skills was mediated by improvements in phonological processing skills.

In a study of older children with identified reading disabilities in grades 3–5, intervention conditions used either the same explicit alphabetic instructional program (articulatory awareness plus synthetic phonics) as in the kindergarten prevention study or an alternative curriculum in which phonics was explicitly taught but in which the emphasis was on reading and writing connected text (Torgesen 1997). These two groups received eighty hours of individualized remediation over an eight-week period. Both groups showed a large improvement in word reading ability, but the more explicit program produced greater gains in phonological decoding skills (as measured by the ability to read pseudowords). At the end of the program, few children in the more explicit program remained poor phonological decoders. The improvements in word-reading accuracy made by children in both groups were accompanied by growth in reading comprehension to the extent that, at the end of the study, the children comprehended written material at a level consistent with their general verbal ability. A remaining concern was that gains in reading fluency were not nearly as dramatic as increases in reading accuracy.

Based on the results of these studies, Torgesen (1997) provided some general principles of instructional programs that are effective with children who have problems with word recognition. Specifically, he suggested that instruction be more explicit and comprehensive since the evidence shows that children who fail to learn to read must be explicitly taught. In addition, he observed that instruction must be more intensive because children with word-level reading problems acquire skills more slowly, need more repetition, and need more experience in different contexts. Finally, instruction must be more supportive at both the emotional and the cognitive level, using encouragement, feedback, and positive reinforcement, because learning is more difficult, proceeds more slowly, and is generally more frustrating.

The State University of New York at Albany
Reading Intervention Studies

Vellutino et al. (1996) identified children who scored below the fifteenth percentile in real-word and pseudoword reading skills at the beginning of the second semester of first grade. These children were selected from schools with a high probability of the children having strong literacy backgrounds (largely middle class and above and predominantly Caucasian). These children received thirty minutes of daily individualized tutoring. Approximately half this tutorial was devoted to explicit code-based activities, as well as word recognition and writing activities; the other half was devoted to activities involving decoding and other strategies for word recognition. At the end of only one semester, approximately 70 percent of the children were reading within or above the average range based on national norms. These results translated to a reading failure rate of approximately 1.5 to 3 percent of the overall population, depending on whether severely impaired and moderately impaired readers were both included in the tally (3 percent) or only severely impaired readers (1.5 percent). Further, children who responded well to remediation, and caught up to their normal reading peers, generally maintained these performance levels once the intervention was discontinued. Most of these children required only one semester of remediation; the children who were still having difficulty when the intervention was discontinued received two semesters of remediation. Thus we see that early intervention helps reduce the number of children who will require protracted remediation to become independent readers and writers; some children, however, will continue to need such services.

In a related study, Scanlon and Vellutino (1996) observed that kindergarten teachers spent much less time on reading practices involving code-based skills relative to time spent on comprehension activities. In classes where kindergarten teachers spent more time on activities that sensitized the children to the phonemic structure of language, students had better reading skills in first grade, particularly if they entered school lacking in rudimentary literacy skills, such as letter identification

The University of Colorado Reading Intervention Studies

Concerns about whether training leads to improvement in reading skills once the intervention is discontinued were confronted in studies from the University of Colorado (Olsen et al. 1997; Wise and Olson 1992, 1995). In an earlier study (Wise and Olson 1992), children with identified reading disabilities in grades 2–6 who were below the local tenth percentile in word recognition skills received an intervention of three to four days a week for approximately thirty minutes during one semester. The intervention, taking advantage of recent advances in the development of speech synthesizers to pronounce words for the child, involved a computer-based program in which children read interesting stories that targeted difficult words. The performance of this group was compared with that of children who remained in their regular remedial classes. After approximately fourteen hours of instruction, the group that received the computer training showed substantially greater gains in phonological awareness skills and word recognition than the standard remediation group. Children with the lowest pretest levels of phoneme awareness, however, gained only half as much as those with higher phoneme awareness, suggesting that explicit training in phoneme awareness might support greater gains in reading.

In a subsequent study (Wise and Olson 1995), second- to fifth-grade children with reading problems were put in groups of three and given training in phoneme awareness similar to some of the training employed by Torgesen et al. (1997). The initial training was grounded in the development of children's awareness of the oral-motor patterns associated with different phonemes (Lindamood and Lindamood 1975). Children then worked on computer programs where they (1) practiced manipulating letter symbols in response to syllables spoken by the computer; (2) explored spelling patterns and print-sound relations through spelling exercises in which the computer pronounced correct and incorrect typed responses; and (3) matched printed pseudowords to pseudowords pronounced by the computer. Children also spent about a third of their twenty-five-hour training time reading stories on the computer with decoding support. This group was compared with a second group that received small-group instruction emphasizing comprehension strategies. The comprehension group spent most of their twenty-five hours reading, a third of the time with stories off the computer and two-thirds of the time with stories and decoding support on the computer.

The results showed that the group receiving explicit training in phonological skills made three times more improvement in phoneme awareness and two times more improvement in pseudoword decoding than the comprehension training group. The phonological group had the advantage on a standardized measure of word recognition without time limits, whereas the comprehension group showed significantly greater gains on a measure requiring rapid recognition of words. There were no significant group differences on the measures of word recognition, however, when children were assessed at one and two years after the intervention was completed, even though the phonological group's pseudoword reading was still significantly better than that of the comprehension group after one year (Olson et al. 1997).

Olson et al. (1997) were concerned that the large and persisting gains in phoneme awareness and phonological decoding would only weakly transfer to gains in word recognition at the end of training and follow-up tests. Some transfer to real-word reading did occur when children had ample time and were encouraged to apply their phonological skills in word recognition during the training period. Apparently, however, the children did not use these skills after training to further accelerate their growth in word recognition. Several explanations for the lack of transfer were considered, including the training period being too short, not enough practice in actual reading skills, and too little focus on issues involving automaticity and speed in phonological processing.

The University of Texas-Houston Health Science Center
Reading Intervention Studies

Foorman et al. (1997a, 1997b, 1998) studied children who were either at risk for reading failure in kindergarten because of social and economic disadvantage, identified with reading disability through special education, or identified as at risk for reading problems and served through Title I programs for children with reduced social and economic circumstances.

In the kindergarten prevention program, the standard kindergarten curriculum was supplemented with activities involving phonological awareness skills for approximately fifteen minutes a day over the school year. Those fifteen minutes led to significant gains in phonological analysis skills relative to children in the same curriculum who did not receive this training (Foorman et al. 1997a).

In another study, children with identified reading disabilities in grades 2 and 3 who were provided services in special education resource rooms received one of two programs in which phonics was taught explicitly. Children in these two groups were compared with a group that received an intervention that involved training to read words on sight (Foorman et al. 1997b). Although children who received one of the phonics programs showed better gains in phonological analysis and word reading skills at the end of one year of intervention, the differences in word reading skills were not apparent when verbal intelligence scores—higher in this group—were controlled in the analysis. In fact, the best predictor of outcomes in all three groups was the child's initial status in word-reading ability, which suggests that the programs were not effective because the child's end-of-year reading ability could be predicted solely on how well he or she read at the beginning of the year. The results of this second study, which contrast with the results from Florida State University and the State University of New York at Albany, may reflect the use of a pullout model in which small groups of children were instructed (Foorman et al. 1997b), rather than receiving instruction in a one-to-one setting. It also may take more intensity to establish the types of gains observed in the Torgesen (1997) and Vellutino et al. (1996) studies.

The third study involved children identified as eligible for

Title I services in eight of ten Title I–eligible schools in the district (Foorman et al. 1997a). These children, who were culturally and linguistically diverse and generally economically disadvantaged, received classroom-level interventions in an attempt to evaluate the degree to which the alphabetic principle must be taught explicitly to facilitate gains in reading skills. The 375 children in the eight schools received classroom-based instruction that involved (1) the district's standard context-based, meaning emphasis instructional program, with staff development and supervision provided by district personnel; (2) a context-based, meaning emphasis approach where professional development and monitoring were provided by research staff; (3) a program in which phonological awareness and phonics skills were taught using letter patterns embedded in the reading material; or (4) a program that included explicit instruction in phonics, applications in reading and writing, and exposure to literature. The analyses in Foorman et al. (1998) involved only the 285 children who received tutorial services; Foorman et al. (1997b) provided preliminary results on the entire sample.

At the end of one school year, the children who received the approach that included explicit phonics instruction with application in literature showed significantly greater gains in word reading and reading comprehension than children who received the other forms of instruction. The results can be seen in figure 3, which shows the growth in word reading over the school year for the four groups. Unfortunately, many children in the other instructional programs—particularly those with poor phonological awareness skills—showed few gains in reading ability. Children who received the combined approach had word reading and reading comprehension skills that approximated national averages at the end of the year. The overall failure rate of children who received this approach represents 5.5 percent of the population from which these children were selected.

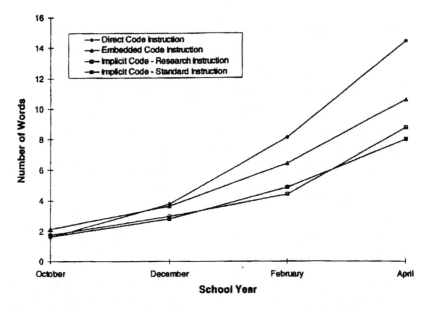

Figure 3.   Growth in word reading scores by curriculum for children in a
Title 1 program. Children who were taught word recognition skills explicitly
(direct code condition) learned more words over the school year than children
who received less explicit instruction. Source: Foorman et al. 1998. Reprinted
with permission of the American Psychological Association.

Conclusions: Intervention Studies

The promising experimental intervention programs described above provide hope for children who read poorly. More
research is needed, including long-term follow-up to see
whether the gains are maintained. Much-needed additional research on identifying specific components of effective programs,
such as the use of decodable versus predictable text and training
in automaticity, is in progress. In many of these studies, phonological awareness training and explicit instruction in phonics
lead to improved word recognition skills. The issue of transfer of
the training results to reading ability independently of the training—apparent in some but not all studies—is clearly important,
however, and requires additional research. This issue is relevant

not only for transfer to real-word reading but also for the development of reading comprehension skills. Skilled reading is more than just efficient decoding. Development of word recognition skills is a necessary but not sufficient condition, for reading proficiency is defined as the ability to *understand* reading materials. Once children develop accurate word recognition skills, they must be able to decode words rapidly; comprehension processes are separable and can be taught. It does not seem reasonable, however, to expect proficiency in comprehension, much less literacy, if the child cannot decode words in isolation or in text.

Studies of Reading Failure Can Improve
Classroom Reading Practices

In considering how studies of reading failure can lead to improved classroom instruction, we must recognize that the intervention studies described in this brief summary have their origins in studies of beginning and skilled readers; thus the principles derived from these studies tend to focus on processes that are part of the early development of reading skills because beginning reading skills are the level at which most poor readers fail. One goal has been to identify where most poor readers have difficulty (i.e., word recognition and phonological awareness skills) and to use that information as the basis for intervention. As the intervention studies show, applying these findings potentially translates to lower failure rates in overall school populations through classroom instruction and tutorial programs.

When NICHD and other research suggesting an important role for explicit instruction in word recognition skills is examined by some reading professionals and the media, arguments arise over whether children should be taught with phonics methods or through meaning-based approaches (Chall 1967, 1983). In general, the NICHD research does not lead to extreme positions on either side of this debate. Most of the NICHD-supported intervention studies employed programs that include important elements from context or meaning-based (so-called whole-language) programs as well as explicit instruction in the alphabetic code. In fact, the NICHD research supports approaches embedded in both phonics and whole-language approaches.

The tendency to interpret the NICHD research, often in the name of "science," as supporting phonics instruction as a panacea for literacy problems is particularly disturbing. For example, materials distributed by the National Right to Read Foundation, as well as a report that purports to summarize NICHD research (Center for the Future of Teaching and Learning 1996), exaggerate the findings of these studies, especially the extent to which the intervention results support the instructional recommendations in the reports. NICHD researchers have used a variety of phonics techniques, often as part of a comprehensive approach to intervention. No NICHD data support a single approach to phonics, much less a specific sequence, number, or set of rules that must be learned, or an essential role for decontextualized drills. We lament the reliance on ideology and invective as opposed to the more difficult task of completing the research that will help educators and policymakers implement effective reading practices. No simple, single message can be obtained from the NICHD research.

The NICHD studies do support a role for instruction in the alphabetic principle, including phonological awareness skills and phonics, as an essential and necessary (but not sufficient) part of early reading instruction. In addition, the research suggests that for children at risk for reading failure or who are poor readers, phonics knowledge should be presented explicitly and in an orderly progression. Such instruction in the early grades may actually prevent reading failure, which is why we feel it should be part of regular classroom practices for all children. In many classroom settings, obtaining this type of instruction is a problem.

As Adams and Bruck (1995) and Pressley and Rankin (1994) point out, however, whole-language practices have come to predominate in regular classroom instruction in reading today for some good reasons. For example, the emphases on meaning, comprehension, writing, and the general philosophy of integrating reading and writing to enhance meaning have had positive influences on literacy instruction. Research evaluating whole-language practices shows that some children, who otherwise might not see a reason to read, learn to enjoy reading and writing when provided with these types of programs. The whole-language movement has increased the quality of literature in schools, provided more emphasis on library resources, and shifted the goal of reading instruction toward meaningfulness and enjoyment. Children and their families are encouraged to spend more time reading and writing, which clearly facilitates improved ability and interest. Positive attitudes toward reading are associated with whole-language practices.

At the same time, some advocates of whole-language practices who are opposed to putting any emphasis on phonological awareness skills, phonics skills, and word recognition processes have done many students a disservice. To illustrate, Goodman (1986) argues that segmenting words to learn to read was unnatural and hindered learning:

> Many school traditions seem to have actually hindered language development. In our zeal to make it easy, we've made it hard. How? Primarily by breaking whole (natural) language up into bite-size, but abstract little pieces. It seemed so logical to think that little children could best learn simple little things. We took apart the language and turned it into words, syllables, and isolated sounds. Unfortunately, we also postponed its natural purpose, the communication of meaning, and turned it into a

set of abstractions unrelated to the needs and experiences of the children we sought to help. (page 7)

This view is not only incorrect but potentially destructive, particularly for the many children at risk for reading failure because of deficits in phonological awareness skills. Pressley and Rankin (1994) discovered that experienced and highly successful teachers, including many who view themselves as whole language teachers, teach phonics, often explicitly, but tend not to rely on commercial phonics programs. Many who espouse the principles of whole language, however, are openly critical of teachers who teach phonics. Indeed, the view put forth by many whole-language proponents—that reading is a process as natural as learning to speak—is inconsistent with contemporary cognitive science.

This inconsistency was clearly outlined in a letter to the commissioner of education in the state of Massachusetts signed by forty well-established scientists from major higher education institutes in Massachusetts, many of whom study language and reading. In that letter, the authors observed that "learning how to decode the speech sounds notated by the writing system ('phonics') is fundamental to reading." The authors also observed that the hypotheses concerning the nature of language central to some whole-language viewpoints are not supported by linguistic research. The authors specifically rejected "the view that the decoding of written words plays a relatively minor role in reading compared to strategies such as contextual guessing. This latter view treats the alphabetic nature of our writing system as little more than an accident, when in fact it is the most important property of written English—a linguistic achievement of historic importance." The state of the science relevant to the role of alphabetic coding in beginning reading was summarized succinctly by Stanovich (1994), who stated

That direct instruction in alphabetic coding facilitates early reading instruction is one of the most well established conclusions in all of behavioral science . . . . Conversely, the idea that learning to read is just like learning to speak is accepted by no responsible linguist, psychologist, or cognitive scientist in the research community. (pp. 285–86)

The most credible solution to reducing reading failure is much like that proposed by Adams (1990) who endorsed a balance between literature-based (meaning oriented) instruction and systematic and explicit instruction in phonological awareness, phonics, and other processes underlying word recognition skills. The extent to which these concepts can be used depends on the level of reading development in an individual child. No reading program is equally beneficial for all children. Successful teachers include elements of code-based instruction with a rich, meaning-based context to develop the skills for reading success.

A major question is how to become a successful teacher of reading. The research summarized in Pressley and Rankin (1994) indicates that teacher preparation is an important component in preventing reading failure. Recent reports have raised concerns about how well teachers are prepared to teach reading, particularly beginning reading and those processes involving language and word recognition skills (Moats and Lyon 1996). These reports have been oriented toward poor readers, and many factors influence outcomes with poor readers that don't involve classroom instruction, such as the amount of time spent on reading, the match of the classroom and the remedial program, and administrative policies (Allington 1991). Many skilled teachers, who often developed their effective approaches to reading instruction after college—through in-service programs, courses, and work with experienced mentors—regard their preparation in reading as inadequate. These issues are important because current evidence shows that effective classroom instruction can prevent reading failure in many children (Blachman 1996, 1997; Foorman et al. 1998).

Conclusions:
Complete Approaches to Reading Instruction

To prevent reading failure, classroom instruction must incorporate what we know about how children learn to read and why children fail to learn to read (Blachman 1996, 1997; Torgesen 1997). As the NICHD research shows, children need to master word recognition skills; many children require explicit instruction in word recognition skills based on early assessments of each child's phonological awareness and reading skills. Such instruction must also be integrated with the rapid processing of words, spelling skills, and reading comprehension skills. This report advocates not an overemphasis on decontextualized phonics but rather an emphasis on developing word recognition skills as part of a complete approach to reading instruction.

The NICHD reading research shows that many children do not develop adequate word recognition skills and thus supports the important role of explicit instruction in phonics and phonological awareness skills. Failure rates of the magnitude we observe today are not acceptable. The intervention studies suggest that these failure rates can be reduced significantly with explicit instruction in word recognition skills as part of a complete reading program, but programs that identify and are applied on a child-by-child basis are expensive. The current magnitude of reading failure is too widespread to permit implementing the programs of the sort employed by Torgesen (1997) and Vellutino et al. (1996) unless the failure rate is initially reduced through effective classroom instruction (Foorman et al. 1998). More research is needed to help develop cost-effective models for early identification, prevention, and intervention. We need to be able not only to distinguish between those who cannot be easily remediated and those who will need prolonged remediation but also to maintain gains in children who respond to intervention.

Learning to read is a lengthy and difficult process for many children, and success is based in large part on developing language and literacy-related skills early in life. Reading failure reflects the lower end of reading proficiency; no qualitative characteristics distinguish the poor reader from the good reader. Since reading failure exists on a continuum, we must provide interventions on a continuum and adjust the emphases as the child develops proficiency.

A massive effort needs to be undertaken to inform parents, and the educational and medical communities, of the need to involve children in reading from the first days of life; to engage children in playing with language through nursery rhymes, storybooks, and writing activities; and, as early as possible, to bring to children the wonder and joy that can be derived from reading. Parents must be aware of the importance of vocabulary development and verbal interactions with their youngsters for enhancing grammar, syntax, and verbal reasoning. In addition, preschool children should be encouraged to learn the letters of the alphabet, to discriminate between letters, to print letters, and to attempt to spell words that they hear. Introducing young children to print will increase their exposure to the purposes of reading and writing, their knowledge of the conventions of print, and their awareness of print concepts.

Reading aloud to children is important for language development (Adams 1990). We must understand, however, that reading to children is not a demonstrably necessary or a sufficient means for teaching reading. Again, the ability to read requires a number of skills that, in many children, must be developed via direct and informed instruction provided by properly prepared teachers. In addition, spending more time reading and writing is key to enhancing literacy levels even in children who are disabled in reading.

Effective instruction early in development may ameliorate the effects of poor preschool literacy experiences. The NICHD prevention and early intervention studies speak to the importance of early identification and intervention with children at risk for reading failure. Procedures now exist to identify such children. This information needs to be widely disseminated to schools, teachers, and parents. Kindergarten programs should be designed so that all children will develop the prerequisite phonological, vocabulary, and early reading skills necessary for success in the first grade. More specifically, beginning reading programs should ensure that adequate instructional time is allotted to the teaching of phonemic awareness skills, phonics skills, and spelling and orthographic skills. As the child develops proficiency with word recognition, reading fluency, automaticity, and comprehension strategies should be emphasized. *All* of these components of reading are *necessary* but *not sufficient* components of a complete approach to reading instruction. For children having difficulty learning to read, it is *imperative* that *each* of these components be taught in an integrated fashion and that ample practice in reading instructional-level material be afforded.

An impediment to serving the needs of children demonstrating difficulties learning to read is current teacher preparation practices in many colleges of education. Many teachers lack basic knowledge and understanding of reading development and the nature of reading difficulties. Major efforts should be undertaken to ensure that colleges of education possess the expertise and commitment to foster expertise in teachers at both preservice and in-service levels. Strong knowledge and skills-based training programs with formal board certification for teachers of reading should be developed.

The sad irony is that we have known about reading development and reading difficulties for more than the past thirty years. The ophthalmologist Hinshelwood, who was one of the earliest students of reading failure, observed, like most of his colleagues at the time, that people who read poorly had problems at the level of the single word—they called it *word-blindness*. He was wrong about the basis of the problem—he thought it was attributable to visual deficits when we now know that reading is a language-based skill and that poor reading is primarily due to language-based difficulties. But Hinshelwood was absolutely correct about the importance of understanding why children do not learn to read and about doing something about reading failure:

> It is a matter of the highest importance to recognize the cause and the true nature of this difficulty in learning to read which is experienced by these children, otherwise they may be harshly treated as imbeciles or incorrigibles and either neglected or flogged for a defect for which they are in no wise responsible. The recognition of the true character of the difficulty will lead the parents and teachers of these children to deal with them in a proper way, not by harsh and severe treatment, but by attempting to overcome the difficulty by patient and persistent training (1902, p. 99).

That is as true today as it was almost a century ago.

References

Adams, M. J. 1990. *Beginning to read*. Cambridge, Mass.: MIT Press.

Adams. M.J., and M. Bruck. 1995. Resolving the "Great Debate." *American Educator* 19: 10–20.

Adams, M. J., R. Treiman, and M. Pressley. 1997. "Reading, writing, and literacy." In I. Siegal and A. Renniger, eds., *Handbook of child psychology*, Vol. 4: *Child psychology in practice*. New York: John Wiley.

Allington, R. L. 1991. Children who find learning to read difficult: School responses to diversity. In E. H. Hiebert, ed., *Literacy for a diverse society*. New York: Teachers College Press.

Ball, E. W., and B. A. Blachman. 1991. Does phoneme awareness training in kindergarten make a difference in early word recognition and developmental spelling? *Reading Research Quarterly* 26: 49–66.

Benton, A. L., and D. Pearl. 1978. *Dyslexia*. New York: Oxford University Press.

Blachman, B. 1996. Preventing early reading failure. In S. C. Cramer and W. Ellis, eds., *Learning disability: Lifelong issues*. Baltimore: Paul C. Brookes.

———. 1997. Early intervention and phonological awareness: A cautionary tale. In Blachman, ed., *Foundations of reading acquisition and dyslexia: Implications for early intervention*. Mahwah, N.J.: Lawrence Erlbaum.

Bradley, L., and P. E. Bryant. 1983. Categorizing sounds and learning to read—a causal connection. *Nature* 301: 419–421.

Brady, S. A., and D. P. Shankweiler, eds. 1991. *Phonological processes in literacy: A tribute to Isabelle Y. Liberman*. Hillsdale, N.J.: Lawrence Erlbaum.

Brown, I. S., and R. H. Felton. 1990. Effects of instruction on beginning reading skills in children at risk for reading disability. *Reading and Writing: An Interdisciplinary Journal* 2: 223–41.

Brown, R., M. Pressley, P. van Meter, and T. Schuder. 1996. A quasi-experimental validation of transactional strategies instruction with low-achieving second-grade readers. *Journal of Educational Psychology* 88: 18–37.

Byrne, B., and R. Fielding-Barnsley. 1995. Evaluation of a program to teach phonemic awareness to young children: A 2- and 3-year follow-up and a new preschool trial. *Journal of Educational Psychology* 87: 488–503.

Cardon, L. R., S. D. Smith, D. W. Fulker, B. S. Kimberling, B. F. Pennington, and J. C. DeFries. 1994. Quantitative trait locus for reading disability on chromosome 6. *Science* 226: 276–79.

Center for the Future of Teaching and Learning. 1996. Thirty years of NICHD research: What is known about how children learn to read. *Effective School Practices* 15: 33–46.

Chall, J. S. 1983. *Learning to read: The Great Debate*. 1967. Reprint, N.Y.: McGraw-Hill.

Felton, R. H. 1993. Effects of instruction on the decoding skills of children with phonological-processing problems. *Journal of Learning Disabilities* 26: 583–89.

Foorman, B. R., D. J. Francis, J. M. Fletcher, C. Schatschneider, and P. Mehta. 1998. The role of instruction in learning to read: Preventing reading failure in at-risk-children. *Journal of Educational Psychology* 90: 37–58.

Foorman, B. R., D. J. Francis, T. Beeler, D. Winikates, and J. M. Fletcher. 1997a. Early interventions for children with reading problems: Study designs and preliminary findings. *Learning Disabilities: A Multi-Disciplinary Journal* 8: 63–71.

Foorman, B. R., D. J. Francis, D. Winikates, P. Mehta, C. Schatschneider, and J. M. Fletcher. 1997b. Early intervention for children with reading disabilities. *Scientific Studies of Reading* 1: 255–76.

Francis, D. J., S. E. Shaywitz, K. K. Stuebing, B. A. Shaywitz, and J. M. Fletcher. 1996. Developmental lag versus deficit models of reading disability: A longitudinal, individual growth curves analysis. *Journal of Educational Psychology* 88: 3–17.

Goodman, K. S. 1986. *What's whole in whole language?* Portsmouth, N.H.: Heinemann.

Gough, P. B., and M. L. Hillinger. 1980. Learning to read: An unnatural act. *Bulletin of the Orton Society* 30: 179–96.

Gough, P. B., and W. E. Tumner. 1986. Decoding, reading, and reading disability. *Remedial and Special Education* 7: 6–10.

Grigorenko, E. L., F. B. Wood, M. S. Meyer, L. A. Hart, W. C. Speed, A. Shuster, and D. L. Pauls. 1997. Susceptibility loci for distinct components of developmental dyslexia on chromosomes 6 and 15. *American Journal of Human Genetics* 60: 27–39.

Hinshelwood, J. 1902. Congenital word blindness, with reports of 10 cases. *Opthalmology Review* 21: 91–99.

Hoover, W. A., and P. B. Gough. 1990. The simple view of reading. *Reading and Writing* 2: 127–60.

Juel, C. 1988. Learning to read and write: A longitudinal study of 54 children from first through fourth grades. *Journal of Educational Psychology* 80: 437–47.

Lerner, J. 1989. Educational intervention in learning disabilities. *Journal of the American Academy of Child and Adolescent Psychiatry* 28: 326–31.

Liberman, A. M. 1996. *Speech: A special code.* Cambridge, Mass.: MIT Press.

――――. 1997. How theories of speech effect research in reading and writing. In B. Blachman, ed., *Foundations of reading acquisition and dyslexia: Implications for early intervention.* Mahwah, N.J.: Lawrence Erlbaum.

Liberman, A. M., F. S. Cooper, D. Shankweiler, and M. Studdert-Kennedy. 1967. Perception of the speech code. *Psychological Review* 74: 731–61.

Liberman, I. Y. 1971. Basic research in speech and lateralization of language: Some implications for reading disability. *Bulletin of the Orton Society* 21: 72–87.

――――. 1973. Segmentation of the spoken word. *Bulletin of the Orton Society* 23: 65–77.

Liberman, I. Y., and A. Liberman. 1992. Whole language versus code emphasis: Underlying assumptions and their implications for reading instruction. In P. B. Gough, L. C. Ehri, and R. Treiman, eds., *Reading acquisition.* Hillsdale, N.J.: Erlbaum.

Liberman, I. Y., D. P. Shankweiler, and A. M. Liberman. 1989. The alphabetic principle and learning to read. In D. P. Shankweiler and I. Y. Liberman, eds., *Phonology and reading disability: Solving the reading puzzle.* IARLD Monograph series. Ann Arbor: University of Michigan Press.

Lindamood, C., and P. Lindamood. 1975. *Auditory discrimination in depth.* Columbus, Ohio: Science Research Associates Division, Macmillan/McGraw Hill.

Lundberg, I., J. Frost, and O. Peterson. 1988. Effects of an extensive program for stimulating phonological awareness in pre-school children. *Reading Research Quarterly* 23: 263–84.

Lyon, G. R. 1995. Research in learning disabilities: Contributions from scientists supported by the National Institute of Child Health and Human Development. *Journal of Child Neurology* 10: S120–S126.

Lyon, G. R., D. Alexander, and S. Yaffe. 1997. Progress and promise in research on learning disabilities. *Learning Disabilities* 8: 1–6.

Lyon, G. R., and L. Moats. 1997. Critical conceptual and methodological considerations in reading intervention research. *Journal of Learning Disabilities* 30: 578–88.

Lyon, G. R., and J. Rumsey, eds. 1997. *Neuroimaging: A window to the neurological foundations of learning and behavior in children.* Baltimore: Paul C. Brookes.

Moats, L. C., and G. R. Lyon. 1996. Wanted: Teachers with knowledge of language. *Topics in Language Disorders* 16: 73–86.

Office of Special Education Programs. 1993. *Implementation of the individuals with disabilities in education act: Fifteenth annual report to Congress.* Washington, D.C.: U.S. Department of Education.

Olson, R. K., and B. W. Wise. 1992. Reading on the computer with orthographic and speech feedback: An overview of the Colorado Remedial Reading Project. *Reading and Writing: An Interdisciplinary Journal* 4: 107–44.

Olson, R. K., B. W. Wise, J. Ring, and M. Johnson. 1997. Computer-based remedial training in phoneme awareness and phonological decoding: Effects on the post-training development of word recognition. *Scientific Studies of Reading* 1: 235–53.

Pressley, M., and J. Rankin. 1994. More about whole language methods of reading instruction for students at risk for early reading failure. *Learning Disabilities Research and Practice* 9: 157–68.

Rayner, K., S. C. Sereono, M. F. Lesch, and A. Pollatsek. 1995. Phonological codes are automatically activated during reading: Evidence from an eye movement priming paradigm. *Psychological Science* 6: 26–31.

Scanlon, D. M., and F. R. Vellutino. 1996. Prerequisite skills, early instruction, and success in first-grade reading: Selected results from a longitudinal study. *Mental Retardation and Developmental Research Reviews* 2: 54–63.

Share, D. L., and K. E. Stanovich. 1995. Cognitive processes in early reading development: A model of acquisition and individual differences. *Issues in Education: Contributions from Educational Psychology* 1: 1–57.

Shaywitz, S. E. 1996. Dyslexia. *Scientific American* 275: 98–104.

Shaywitz, S. E., M. D. Escobar, B. A. Shaywitz, J. M. Fletcher, and R. Makuch. 1992. Evidence that dyslexia may represent the lower tail of the normal distribution of reading ability. *New England Journal of Medicine* 326: 145–50.

Shaywitz, S. E., B. A. Shaywitz, J. M. Fletcher, and M. D. Escobar. 1990. Prevalence of reading disability in boys and girls: Results of the Connecticut Longitudinal Study. *Journal of the American Medical Association* 264: 998–1002.

Stanovich, K. E. 1994. Romance and reality. *Reading Teacher* 4: 280–90.

Torgesen, J. K. 1997. The prevention and remediation of reading disabilities: Evaluating what we know from research. *Journal of Academic Language Therapy* 1: 11–47.

Torgesen, J. K., R. K. Wagner, C. A. Rashotte, A. W. Alexander, and T. Conway. 1997. Preventative and remedial interventions for children with severe reading disabilities. *Learning Disabilities: A Multi-Disciplinary Journal* 8: 51–62.

Vellutino, F. R. 1979. *Dyslexia: Theory and research.* Cambridge, Mass.: MIT Press.

————. 1991. Introduction to three studies on reading acquisition: Convergent findings on theoretical foundations of code-oriented versus whole-language approaches to reading instruction. *Journal of Educational Psychology* 83: 437–43.

Vellutino, F. R., D. M. Scanlon, E. Sipay, S. Small, A. Pratt, R. Chen, and M. Denckla. 1996. Cognitive profiles of difficult-to-remediate and readily remediated poor readers: Early intervention as a vehicle for distinguishing between cognitive and experiential deficits as basic causes of specific reading disability. *Journal of Educational Psychology* 88: 601–38.

Wise, B. W., and R. K. Olson. 1992. Spelling exploration with a talking computer improves phonological coding. *Reading and Writing* 4: 145–56.

————. 1995. Computer-based phonological awareness and reading instruction. *Annals of Dyslexia* 45: 99–122.

Appendix

Selected NICHD Studies of Normal Reading Development and Reading Disorders

Research Topic (NR) = Normal Reading (RD) = Reading Disorders		Principal Investigator
Reading Disability and Early Language Impairments	(RD)	D.M. Aram
Prevention and Treatment of Reading Disabilities	(RD)	V.W. Berninger
Handwriting, Spelling and Composition Skills	(NR/RD)	V.W. Berninger
Development of Reading Curricula for LD Children	(RD)	V.W. Berninger

Teacher Training in Reading Development and
   Disorders   (NR/RD)   V.W.Berninger
Gestures as Phonological Units   (NR)   C. Best
The Speech Mode and Its Early Development   (NR)   C. Best
Phonologically-Based Remediation for RD
   Students   (RD)   B.A. Blachman
Development of Word Recognition Processes   (NR)   J.R. Booth
Colored Computer Displays Effects on Reading   (NR/RD)   L.H. Boyd
The Role of Phonological Representation in
   Phonological Awareness and Literacy   (NR/RD)   S. Brady
Phonological Processes in Sentence
   Comprehension   (NR)   S. Crain
Neuroimaging Analysis of Reading Disability   (RD)   J.S. Duncan
EEG Studies of Disabled Readers   (RD)   R.A. Dykman
fMRI of Phonological and Sensory Processing in
   Dyslexia   (RD)   G.F. Eden
Analytic Processes Unique to Phonology   (NR)   L. Feldman
Behavioral Definition and Subtyping of Dyslexia   (RD)   F. Wood
A Longitudinal Study of Normal Reading
   Development   (NR)   D. Flowers
Early Interventions for Children At-Risk for RD   (RD)   B. Foorman
Phonological Development and Development of
   Literacy   (NR)   A. Fowler
Phonetic Gestures and Their Perceptions   (NR)   C. Fowler
Language Comprehension and Reading   (NR)   L. Frazier
Cognitively Based Treatments of Acquired
   Dyslexia   (RD)   R. Friedman
Acquired Dyslexia or Alexia After Stroke   (RD)   M. Friend
Cross-Domain Comprehension Processes   (NR)   P.J. Holcomb
Brain Morphology and Dyslexia   (RD)   G.W. Hynd
Epidemiology of Learning Disability   (RD)   S.K. Katusic
Common Phonology of Speech and Reading   (NR)   L. Katz
Interactive Reading/Spelling and
   Comprehension Software   (NR/RD)   P. Lindamood
Phonological Effects in the Lexical Access of
   Words   (NR)   G. Lukatela
Perceptual, Linguistic and Computational Bases
   of Dyslexia   (RD)   F.R. Manis
Examining the Strategic Processing Of Text   (NR)   S.M. Mannes
Syntactic Processes in Reading Development   (NR)   L. Maurais
Teacher Training for Reading Intervention   (NR/RD)   D. McCutcheon
Neonatal Predictors of Later Language and
   Reading Development   (NR/RD)   D.L. Molfese
Acoustic Structure of Speech to Young Children   (NR)   J.L. Morgan
Treatment of Developmental Reading Disabilities   (RD)   R.D. Morris

Schooling and Cognitive Development: A Natural Experiment	(NR)	F.J. Morrison
Language and Literacy in Bilingual Children	(NR)	D.K. Oller
Reading and Language Processes	(NR/RD)	R K. Olson
Computer-Based Remediation of Reading Disabilities	(RD)	R.K. Olson
Computer-Speech Feedback for Dyslexic Children	(RD)	R.K. Olson
rCBF and Behavior: Adult and Second Generation Dyslexia	(RD)	D.L. Pauls
Comprehensive Test of Phonological Awareness	(NR/RD)	A.A. Pearson
Social Relationships and Early Literacy Development	(NR)	A.D. Pelligrini
Linguistic Phenotype in Familial Dyslexia	(RD)	B.F. Pennington
Brain Morphometry and Reading-Disabled Twins	(RD)	B.F. Pennington
Language, Learning Ability and Language Development	(NR)	S. Pinker
Genetic Contributions to Learning Disability Subtypes	(RD)	W. Raskind
Foveal and Parafoveal Codes in Reading	(NR)	K. Rayner
Language Processing During Reading	(NR)	K. Rayner
Perceptual and Cognitive Processes in Reading	(NR)	K. Rayner
Emergence of Literacy in Sociocultural Context	(NR)	R. Serpell
Distribution and Typology of RD	(RD)	B. Shaywitz
Developmental Phonological Disorders	(RD)	L. Shriberg
Shape Bias in Children's Word Learning	(NR)	L.B. Smith
Genetic Linkage Analysis for Dyslexia	(RD)	S.D. Smith
Coordinating Information in Sentence Processing	(NR)	M. Tannenhaus
Prevention and Remediation of RD	(RD)	J.K. Torgesen
Phonological Processes in Reading Individual Words	(NR)	M.T. Turvey
Preventing Experientially-Based Reading Disability	(RD)	F. Vellutino
Reading-Related Phonological Processes	(NR/RD)	R.K. Wagner
Information Processing in LD Children	(NR/RD)	P.H. Wolff
Physiological Measures of Dyslexia	(RD)	F.B. Wood

Bill Honig

Preventing Failure in
Early Reading Programs

A Summary of Research and Instructional Best Practice

During the past decade the most respected educational and cognitive researchers, the most effective practitioners, and the members of the scientific and medical communities reached agreement on the basic principles of how proficient readers read and the most productive methods of helping children become proficient readers. A convergence of reading theory, evidence, and classroom and school experience has produced a number of critical elements that should guide any reading program. These elements draw from the whole-language movement but also include organized skill development components using those ideas from both traditions that have proved successful and discarding those that have proved ineffective.

Best Practices Help Children Read
Grade-Appropriate Material

Preliminarily, an elementary reading program grounded in best practice should enable 85–90 percent of the students to read and understand grade-appropriate material starting in mid–first grade. With proper instruction and activities, students should by third grade be fluent enough in word recognition, decoding, and passage understanding to be able to read and understand extensive amounts of the more complex and difficult fourth-grade material, regardless of their socioeconomic or language status. By the time students leave elementary school they should

- Read fluently enough to be able to understand the textbooks, informational texts, and novels that will be part of the next year's curriculum
- Have read a large number of books, magazines, and informational text
- Enjoy and be able to learn from reading

Although a comprehensive approach based on proven research and best practice is not currently driving instruction in most classrooms, teachers are hungry for information about specifics and willing to apply them in their classrooms and schools. Reading instruction is ripe for improvement because teachers, daily facing children who are not learning to read, realize there is a gap in instruction. In such a situation, administrative leadership is crucial to crystallizing the potential for improvement.

Before change can occur, educators need a more detailed knowledge of the reading process so that they do not get misled by specious advice. Because most children learn to read in kindergarten and first grade, the best place to begin searching for remedies is observing students who have difficulty reading in upper grades. I have asked more than ten thousand teachers and administrators in this country to describe such students; they uniformly state (consistent with the research) that reading-disabled children in the upper primary grades exhibit

- Poor decoding skills (students struggle with too many individual words and do not know how to tackle a new word effectively)

- A weak vocabulary

- The inability to read strategically and actively

- Poor spelling

- Not having read enough

- Poor motivation, confidence, or avoidance behavior stemming from too much reading failure

Recent research has developed a powerful explanatory theory of why poor readers exhibit such behaviors. According to researchers such as Robert Calfee from Stanford University, this theory is based on the concept that proficient readers get meaning from text in two ways: (1) from the *word*, the vocabulary concept underlying an individual word, and (2) from the *passage*, stringing those words together and thinking about their meaning. For proficient readers, the word recognition part is an automatic, unconscious, and rapid process. We look at the word *idiosyncratic*, and its meaning immediately and effortlessly pops into our consciousness. Conversely, passage understanding is primarily an active, engaged, thinking process, weaving the concepts of individual words into a meaningful whole, thinking about what the author is saying, and connecting it to other ideas.

If readers take too much time and effort decoding individual words, they cannot attend to passage meaning: the rule of thumb is that if the student does not recognize eighteen or nineteen out of twenty words automatically, comprehension suffers. Additionally, by sixth grade if students are reading below approximately 120 words a minute (usually because they are not fluent with many of the words in the text), they probably cannot attend to meaning. The 1992 National Assessment of Educational Programs (NAEP) sample showed that more than 40 percent of

American fourth graders read too slowly to understand what they were reading.

A balanced reading program should include strategies to develop both automatic word recognition and passage comprehension. Many of the current reading programs, however, are based on philosophies that deemphasize the word side *and the tools by which students become automatic with a growing number of words* and overrely on the passage side. Those programs are based on the theory that the difficult task of developing word recognition skills can be avoided or minimized for many children because the passage can supply word meaning. Vast amounts of research and experience dispute this view.

One strand of studies, computer eye research, has disposed of the claims that proficient readers skip large number of words; they actually read virtually every word (at the rate of about one-fifth of a second per word) and see all the letters in each word. (Try skipping a *not* in expository text.) In the sentence *Virtually every word is important or else it wouldn't be there,* only the *is* and the *it* can be left out without masking the meaning of the sentence. Similarly, a difference of one letter in many English words completely changes the meaning of the word (e.g., *sit, sat, set*).

Other studies show that context or meaning strategies can help decode words only about 10–25 percent of the time, that such strategies are too slow for fluency, and that it is the poorer readers who rely on such context-based strategies. Finally, studies have demonstrated that using indirect methods first and waiting to directly instruct those who fail to intuit the alphabetic system significantly decreases the odds that those struggling students will learn to read properly.

In first grade recognizing individual words contributes about 70 percent of meaning (the words and concepts of the story are simple, and if the words are recognized the meaning of the story is apparent). In later grades other factors, such as strategic reading ability or the ability to discuss what has been read, increase in importance, but recognizing individual words still remains crucial to reading for understanding. This chapter focuses on the skills necessary for developing automatic word recognition for a growing number of words; other techniques, such as reading to children and discussion, writing, and motivational strategies, are also essential components of a successful reading program but are not discussed here.

The Critical Importance of Decoding

Automatically reading a growing number of individual words depends on knowing how to use the alphabetic system to decode a word the first few times it is read. (Alphabetic decoding in the early primary grades, when students know the meaning of almost all the words being read, is the ability to read through a word from left to right, generate the sounds that are connected to all the letters or letter patterns in that word, and manipulate those sounds until they connect to a word in the student's speaking vocabulary.) *First-grade decoding ability predicts 80–90 percent of reading comprehension in second and third grade and still accounts for nearly 40 percent of reading comprehension by ninth grade.* Thus, equipping each child with the ability to decode simple words should be a major goal of kindergarten and early first-grade reading instruction.

Why should the ability to sound out a rarely used word like *pad* or a pseudoword (a pseudoword assures that the child has not seen and memorized the word and so is a true test of decoding ability) such as *mot* in mid–first grade and *lote* or *blar* by late first grade be so predictive of later reading ability? The reason is that the words are stored efficiently in memory for subsequent rapid retrieval. Thoroughly decoding a word the first few times it is read forces a reader to connect the letter/sound combinations to the meaning of the word. When a word such as *cat* is read, the letters of the word (the *c*, the *a*, and the *t*) are stored in one part of the brain, the sounds (the /*k*/, the /*a*/, and the /*t*/) in another, and the meaning of the word (a furry animal that purrs) in another, so that neuronic connections are established among these parts. Subsequent successful readings (about four to fourteen times for most early primary children) strengthen these mental connections and quicken the retrieval process until it is automatic. Sometimes one sound attaches to more than one letter such as in the word *will*, and by second grade students are also storing words by larger chunks such as the /*ate*/ sound in *late*.

Early readers who want to read independently for meaning also need a successful strategy for figuring out words that they have not yet seen in print. Even in first grade, readers encounter a large number of words that are in their speaking vocabulary but not yet recognized in print. Since, in the early grades, students must develop a growing number of automatically recognized words, the ability to decode becomes the best predictor of reading comprehension. If students cannot decode simple words by mid–first grade, they will have difficulty developing a growing corpus of automatically recognized words and thus not keep up with grade-appropriate texts.

Theories that question the importance of alphabetic decoding have not withstood scientific and empirical scrutiny, and lacking the ability to figure out the sounds of printed words is implicated in most cases of reading deficiency. Compared with full alphabetic screening of a word, other methods cannot retrieve the huge numbers of words in English fast enough—there are too many words to memorize without using the generative nature of the alphabetic system. Contextual cues are essential for increasing vocabulary, for resolving ambiguity in decoded words, or for confirming a decoded word ("Does it make sense or does it sound right?"). But context-driven decoding, even if aided by partial alphabetic clues, is too slow and unreliable to serve as a fluent decoding tool.

For example, a large-scale study in New Zealand[1] found that first-grade students who used sounding-out strategies for new words as opposed to context-based strategies (skipping the word, reading to the end of the sentence, etc.) read significantly better in second and third grades and that the more vulnerable children (those who are poor or learning English as a second language) tended to use the less effective context-based method.

Some educators claim that, since English has so many irregular words, phonics does not work. English linguistic patterns, however, are much more regular than believed. According to Foorman, about 50 percent of English words are completely regular, about 37 percent are regular except for one vowel that is usually close (*put*), and 13 percent are irregular but still contain many regular patterns (*ocean*). More important, regularity is not the issue; being able to sequentially generate sounds for all the letters or letter patterns in regular and irregular words and forge those sounds into a word, which is crucial for later instant retrievability, is. (A reader still must map the /*ite*/ sound in *light* to the letters *ight*.) Regularity determines how generalizable the pattern is, not the necessity for mapping letters and sounds. In sounding out words students only need to get close enough to the sounds so that the mind can put the sounds together to make a recognizable word.

Does Decoding Have to Be Taught?

Extensive research and practical experience have demonstrated that learning to read does not come as naturally to most

1. W. Tunmer and J. Chapman (1996).

children as learning to speak does—it needs to be taught. Although as many as 50 percent of children will intuit the alphabetic system from the instructional strategies now in vogue—exposure to print and print activities and minilessons in the context of reading a story—a significant number of students (especially those who are dyslexic, of low socioeconomic background, and learning English as a second language who are currently failing under our present emphasis on indirect strategies) need an organized program that teaches phonemic awareness, letter-sound correspondences, and decoding skills to learn to read.

Although many first-grade students may seem to be progressing because they are memorizing words, they are unable to decode (and will subsequently suffer reading problems). Because all students will benefit from help in consolidating alphabetic knowledge, they need to be evaluated to determine if they understand and can use the alphabetic system.

Decoding ability, vocabulary level, and spelling are highly correlated with reading comprehension. Pedagogically, they are connected. The best method for expanding one's vocabulary is to read extensively, and children cannot read extensively, especially when text becomes conceptually and structurally more difficult in third and fourth grade, unless they know a large number of words automatically and are proficient at decoding and learning new words. Similarly, learning spelling patterns helps accelerate decoding and developing automaticity with written words.

Perfecting the decoding tool and becoming automatic with enough words to be able to read fourth-grade materials fluently usually take two to three years of practice in first, second, and third grades. When combined with strategic reading abilities, they allow third graders to be ready for the more difficult fourth-grade materials. Similarly, learning the spelling patterns in words and their underlying phonological and morphemic structure assists in reading fluency and word attack skills.

Extensive reading (combined with appropriate skill, writing, and oral language instruction) is a necessary strategy for developing sufficient vocabulary, becoming automatic with an increasing number of words, perfecting the ability to decode new words, increasing comprehension ability, and connecting to the ideas, concepts, and realities of the world so that students are able to read at their grade level. Unfortunately, in the later elementary grades the average U.S. student reads less than half the number of words necessary for grade-level comprehension.[2] For example, a fifth-grade student should be reading between a million and a half to two million words a year (about twenty-five minutes a day in school and twenty minutes a night, four nights a week, at home). Only the top quarter of students reads this much. The average fifth-grade student reads only 600,000 words, less than half of what is necessary. Poor readers may read as little as 100,000 words a year, or only 5 percent of what they need to read. No wonder they fall behind.

Starting at fourth grade, texts contain large numbers of new and difficult words that appear infrequently. For example, at fifth grade a million words of running text will contain about forty thousand words that appear only once or twice. Most of these words carry the essential meaning of a passage, especially in expository text, and form the corpus of words students need to learn to keep vocabulary learning on target. Using context to figure out the meaning of words will work about 10 percent of the time; thus, a student who reads approximately two million words a year will figure out the meaning of about eight thousand new words and will remember approximately half of them, or about four thousand words a year. Literate high school graduates need to know some 60,000–80,000 words (including proper names and idioms).

2. R. Andersen (1992).

Beginning students have speaking vocabularies of about five thousand words (students from low socioeconomic backgrounds may have considerably fewer), but all must learn about four thousand words a year, or about seventy words a week during the thirteen years of schooling. While direct vocabulary instruction can teach approximately ten words a week, the bulk of vocabulary growth after the third grade must come from extensive reading (about twenty-five minutes a day in school and twenty minutes a night four nights a week at home). For preparing students to read this extensively, they need equipping with the proper reading tools and assuring fluent and effortless use of those tools.

Is Decoding Necessary for All First-Graders?

Every child needs to be able to analyze and connect the letters and sounds of words to read fluently. Some intuit how to sound out words; most children need to be taught. (Deaf children typically read significantly below grade level; those who read proficiently have figured out a substitute system to detect patterns in words.)

Research has shown that decoding and independent reading of simple, nonpredictive texts in first grade is developmentally appropriate (approximately 95 percent of children are mature enough to learn basic phonemic awareness and letter recognition in kindergarten and phonics and decoding in first grade). These studies have also found that, if students are not taught these skills early, most will never recover. Estimates are that only one out of eight children not reading at grade level by the end of first grade will ever read grade-appropriate materials (expensive and well-designed interventions can improve these odds).

Decoding gives students a sense of success, confidence, and independence in figuring out and remembering a new word and thus leads to students' knowing they can look at previously un-read simple text and read it. Nondecoders seldom experience this success and thus become frustrated in attempting to read. Researchers estimate that nearly half of special education students would not need that expensive program if they had been taught to read properly initially. Unfortunately, few schools make decoding a primary objective in first grade, check to see which children can do it, and then help the ones who cannot.

Instructional Implications

To acquire the ability to decode a simple word by mid–first grade, students must have

- Basic levels of phonemic awareness (the ability to hear and manipulate the sounds in spoken words)
- An ability to recognize letters
- Acquired basic concepts in print
- Learned about half the basic letter-sound correspondences (at least the consonants and short vowels and a smattering of blends, long vowels, and more complex vowels) and the patterns of words using these sounds
- Learned a core of high-frequency words and phonograms, how to map sounds to letter-letter patterns in sequence in written words (blending or sounding out), and thus how to figure out a word that has not been read before but is in the student's speaking vocabulary

Many students figure out how to sound out or blend after a few attempts; many others find this skill difficult and need to be taught over a period of several months. In late first and second grades students need to extend their letter-sound knowledge to the more complex patterns and learn to use larger orthographic patterns when they sound out a word.

Graphophonemic Cueing

Once students understand the concept of a word in print (the partial or prealphabetic stage usually accomplished in kinder-garten) and that words start and end with specific letters (spelling *some sm*), they are ready to move to the alphabetic stage (knowing that syllables contain a vowel and that all sounds must be accounted for—they might spell *some* as *som*) and learn how to use phonics to decode a word. In this stage they must learn to look at all the letters or letter patterns in the word in sequence, generate a potential sound from each of those including the vowels, and manipulate those sounds until they become a recognizable word. Only by connecting letters and letter patterns and their sounds will they be able to store that written word in memory so that after several successful readings it becomes immediately retrievable and thus automatically recognized (a sight word).

Many students learn to sound out words in a short time; about a third need extensive assistance in learning to blend. Current methods discourage those students from learning to sound out words thoroughly and legitimize remaining in the first/last letter and guess stage. As explained above, partial storage (using the first or last letters or parts of the word) forces students to slow down for context checks, resulting in slow retrievability. Thus, those students who, in the partial-cueing or prealphabetic stage in which they were trying to develop the concept of a word and used skipping and guessing strategies in conjunction with first and last letter cues, must now learn to stay with all the letters of a written word and generate all the sounds of the word until the meaning of the word becomes conscious. In other words, they must be weaned from reliance on the context and syntactic cues used in kindergarten pretend reading and learn how to screen words visually (context cues are still important to resolve ambiguity, check for accuracy after the word is phonologically decoded, and supply word meaning if the word is not in the student's speaking vocabulary). Using context cues too quickly at this stage in conjunction with first and last letters becomes a crutch or a release that prevents many children from learning the skill of thorough word screening. Instruction should thus encourage students to stay with the word, and reading materials should possess many words that are decodable and match the progress in letter-sound knowledge of the child (decodable text).

Currently, there are four major deficiencies in instruction that prevent students from learning to decode:

1. Nearly 20 percent of students do not develop threshold levels of phonemic awareness in kindergarten (meaning that they cannot distinguish the discrete sounds in words and manipulate and sequence them, which is necessary to connect sounds and letters in words) and are not diagnosed or given assistance.

2. Students are not taught enough about the main letter-sound correspondences and thus do not learn the alphabetic system.

3. About a third of students have difficulty, when first encountering a word, learning how to read through it or sound it out and have not been taught how to do so.

4. Students have not had the opportunity to practice reading (and rereading) a large number of words based on the early letter-sound patterns in books and so do not auto-

matically know many words. They also have not had enough practice spelling and manipulating words.

Phonemic Awareness

One important breakthrough in the reading field has been discovering how important being able to hear and manipulate the discrete parts of words—phonemic awareness—is in learning to read. Most phonemic awareness comes in learning how print maps to sound in phonics instruction; however, threshold levels are also important. If a child cannot tell what the last sound in *cat* is, she or he will be unable to connect that sound with the written symbol *t* or to read through a word keeping the letters and sounds in proper sequence.

Most children acquire basic phonemic awareness in kindergarten through such activities as rhyming and sound word games. Unfortunately, about a sixth of our children have phonological wiring problems; without special assistance (about twelve to fourteen hours from mid-kindergarten on) they will not acquire basic phonemic awareness. Many of these children end up in special education or Title I programs; many others flounder but remain undetected. Thus, kindergarten programs must identify and assist those children who without intervention will have difficulty learning to read.

One reason for the growth of the whole-language movement was that many children seemed unable to learn phonics and decoding, and thus other ways for them to learn to read were tried. As mentioned earlier, those other ways (predictions using context and first-letter cues) are slow and inaccurate, and teaching children to rely on them produced large numbers of poor readers. Now we know that one main reason many of these students did not learn to decode was that they could not hear and abstract

the sounds; thus we must ensure that children are properly prepared to learn phonics and decoding.

Direct and Systematic Phonics Instruction

Most children need an organized program that directly
teaches the basic consonant-vowel combinations and that follows principles of linguistic sequencing (e.g., words based on
short vowel patterns and simple consonants in early first grade
and then the more complicated vowel marker patterns [*e*-con-
trolled, *r*-controlled, and vowel combinations] and consonant
blends and digraphs [*ch*]). Those basic high-frequency words
that cannot be sounded out also need to be taught in some sequence.

Many children will learn to read by being immersed in text
and having teachers point out letter-sound correspondences in
the context of reading a passage. But research and practice demonstrate that many children never develop an understanding of
the letter-sound alphabetic system through these indirect methods; a recent study showed that about twice as many students
learned to read under systematic instruction compared with the
indirect strategy.[3] All children need to be able to understand and
apply the basic elements of the alphabetic system.

Explicitly teaching letter-sound correspondences introduces
each of the major forty-plus sound components and their graphic
representations in a sequence that progresses from linguistically
easy to linguistically hard (consonants, short vowels, beginning
and ending consonant blends, digraphs, long vowels, other
vowel sounds [*aw, oo, ow,* etc.], complex vowels and dipthongs,
r- and *l*-controlled vowels). The sequence also includes teaching

---

3. B. Foorman et al. (1997)—systematic phonics instruction, with whole
language twice as effective as book-driven indirect methods with Title I children.

basic high-frequency words in order from easier to harder, some simple syllabication, and suffix knowledge (e.g., endings such as *ed* and *ing* and the ambiguous letters such as *c* and *y*, etc.). For most children it takes approximately a year, or a hundred lessons, to cover these elements, and most can handle about three new sound-symbols a week. Each phonics lesson (high-frequency words are taught differently but still require decoding in the sense of matching letters or patterns of letters to sound) helps children hear the sound, see the letter-letter pattern representation in words, blend the letter-sounds to make words, and read words with those patterns.

After each lesson demonstrating a particular sound-symbol correspondence, students must be given an opportunity to read words with those sound-letter patterns (or the high-frequency words) in a text with a large percentage of decodable words, engage in wordplay building and sorting words, spell words, and see phonics patterns in the stories they read. Implicit strategies (reading a book and pointing out letter-sound correspondences) should be included as part of any good reading program, but many students will not intuit the alphabetic system without an organized, systematic strand of instruction.

During early first grade, as children learn about how print maps to sound in easy consonant, short vowel, consonant words (*cvc*), they will also learn to generalize from those simple correspondences to other words containing the same combinations even if they have not learned that particular word. Knowing the short vowel sound and the *cvc* pattern of *not* helps them decode *top*. Although many students become confused trying to generalize from the complicated array of patterns that occur in non-controlled text, they will learn (but not be able to generalize from) some individual words representing letter-sound combinations they will not study until later, such as the word *saw*.

Decodable Text

The sound-symbol correspondences (and high-frequency words) must be practiced and reinforced extensively in connected or decodable text. These stories contain large numbers of words that are easy to read because they represent previously taught patterns. Research has shown that the type of text being read by children in the first grade is as important as the method of instruction. Pedagically sound texts can greatly assist students in learning the alphabetic system, which is essential to learning to read.

Yet much of the materials used for teaching reading in first grade are either highly predictable, with too few decodable words and thus not effective for developing independent decoding skills, or contain too many difficult words and are thus too hard and confusing for many children. In predictable books the lack of decodable words stymies many children and encourages overreliance on context and syntax. (They remain, however, a good tool for motivating and reinforcing students who have not yet reached the alphabetic stage and are working on recognizing what a word is in print—a stage that must be reached before thorough word attack strategies and blending can be learned.)

Spelling and Word Manipulation

Finally, activities that allow students to spell and manipulate words by sorting, building, and changing them (changing *sit* to *set* to *sat*) are an essential part of the curriculum. Getting students to pay attention to and play with the structure of words will help many understand the alphabetic principle. For example, individual and class diaries of discoveries about how words work (an *e* at the end of a word makes the vowel say its name; an *r* changes the sound of the vowel before it) are useful techniques.

Studies have shown that programs that incorporate all these elements (as well as reading to children, discussions, and language-rich activities) are about twice as effective as the more indirect or unfocused methods currently in use.

Dynamic and Comprehensive Instruction

Another reason for the growth of whole language-approaches that deemphasized decoding was the sterile and unproductive nature of much phonics instruction (worksheets and paucity of connected text) and the lack of motivational and authentic reading experiences accompanying skills instruction. The decoding instruction being advocated today is much more akin to a thinking phonics program, which strives for an understanding of the alphabetic principle and uses engaging activities to help students learn. In the latest synthesis, decoding instruction is part of a broader language arts curriculum that stresses reading to children, writing, shared reading activities, and discussing literature.

Ongoing Diagnostics

The important benchmarks in learning to phonologically decode and to read for meaning include determining if children have mastered the concept of word, whether they are learning to scan a word and match sound and symbol, which letter-sound correspondences they have mastered, and how effectively they are learning word attack skills. It is almost impossible to acquire this information from whole-class instruction. Additionally, many whole-class shared reading exercises are too difficult for some students and too easy for others. Tailoring instruction for particular skills components is necessary for effective instruction. Skill groups are not the same as tracking. Membership of skill groups changes often as skills are learned, and skill groups occupy only a portion of classroom time.

Lack of Progress

If, by mid-kindergarten, after general class instruction in rhyming and word play, children have not acquired basic levels of phonemic awareness (they cannot tell you the first sound in the spoken word *sat*), they are probably not going to progress without specific interventions and will have difficulty learning phonics (and thus reading) in first grade. About one-sixth of kindergartners will need twenty minutes a day of extra phonemic awareness assistance for about a third of the year to enable them to learn phonics. Similarly, if students have not learned basic decoding skills (the ability to figure out simple *cvc* words), the teacher needs to give these children additional assistance. Thus, a system of diagnostics and intensification is required for students to attain the key components of reading. For those students still not reading, a tutoring/intervention program is important.

A Comprehensive Reading Strategy

The consensus that has developed on the program components necessary to reduce reading failure and improve reading performance is that no one single program will suffice. Best-practice literature points to ten major interventions, all of which must be effectively organized and integrated in an elementary reading program if that school is to have 85–90 percent of students reading grade-appropriate material from end of first grade on. The absence or ineffectiveness of any one of these components will lower the number of students who will be able to handle grade-appropriate materials; thus it is the cumulative effect of these elements that produces high literacy rates. Some of these strands are ongoing; some are appropriate for a particular time:

1. A prekindergarten to fifth-grade (or ending elementary grade level) oral language program in which children are read to at a little above their reading level and ideas discussed.

2. A kindergarten to fifth-grade writing program stressing both narrative and expository writing starting with language experience activities, temporary spelling, process writing strategies, accepted standards for different kinds of writing (telling a story, organizing a report, arguing a point, etc.), and using writing as a means of discussing important ideas.

3. Teaching each child to decode phonologically. Equipping each student with this tool (preferably by mid–first grade) requires

- A kindergarten skills development program of basic phonemic awareness (hearing and manipulating sounds in spoken words), upper- and lower-case letter recognition, and concepts in print, especially recognizing a word in print. A supplemental phonemic awareness program for those children not making progress by midkindergarten.

- A late kindergarten/first-grade strand of organized and systematic phonics to teach students how the alphabetic system works including the letter-sound correspondence system, automatically recognizing a sufficient number of words, and developing enough proficiency in word attack skills (sounding out, seeing common letter patterns: seeing that *sight* is like *light*, seeing parts of words, and generating and selecting from legitimate alternative pronunciations such as reading *bread*) to start to read beginning materials independently in which only about one in twenty words needs to be figured out.

- Using decodable text to practice and perfect the recognition of words based on taught patterns and using spelling and word-building activities.

- Most children should be able to read and understand nonpredictable beginning materials by mid–first grade; some will require more time, others will have mastered these skills and be reading (not pretend reading) by late kindergarten. Children should enhance these skills during late first and second grade.

4. A diagnostic ongoing assessment component to know which children are progressing and which need more intensive instruction. (Students who have learned to decode will get eighteen, nineteen, or twenty words right on a mid–first grade standard decoding test of simple pseudowords [*mot*]; students who don't understand the alphabetic system will get none, one, or two right.) A tutoring or intervention program that assists students in kindergarten, first, and later grades who, after intensified assistance by the teacher, are still not making progress.

5. An independent reading program that gets students to read predictable, decodable, and simple trade books in first grade; at the end of first grade students should be reading some twenty-five to thirty-five narrative and informational books a year. (Fifth-grade students need to read more than a million words of text outside school assignments [approximately twenty minutes a night four nights a week] to learn enough vocabulary words to stay grade-appropriate readers.)

6. An advanced skill development support in syllabication,

word roots, fluency, complex letter-sound correspondences, and mechanics from second grade on.

7. A comprehension development program that includes (1) teaching strategic reading (i.e., summarizing, predicting, questioning, etc.) especially for expository text (emphasized in third through fifth grades) and (2) discussion or book club groups.

8. Vocabulary instruction in word webs, word choice, and word histories.

9. A developmental (linguistically based) spelling program starting in late first or early second grade.

10. A parent and community involvement component that encourages reading to children, having children read to them, and turning off the TV for a nightly reading period.

In the early primary grades enough time for both skill and language-rich activities must be allocated (at least two to three hours a day, including reading in the subject matter areas in early primary); in addition, schools need to purchase a good mix of good literature (including both narrative and informational text), predictable text, and decodable text and ensure that the support programs, such as Title I, special education, and tutoring, are integrated into the reading program right from the start. Teachers should also use a diagnostic approach to know which children are making satisfactory progress, which are not, and doing something to correct the deficiencies quickly.

Learning English as a Second Language

Some educators question whether these principles are generalizable to children learning English as a second language, but in alphabetic languages all children learn to read using the same principles. In Spanish bilingual programs, since the language is more regular and the syllables short, most children should be cracking the code by late kindergarten (some of the most effective Spanish bilingual reading programs now include both syllable/consonant-driven phonics instruction—*mi, ma, mu, bi, ba, bu*—with vowel-driven instruction—*ma, ba, pa*—as well as the interchangeability of individual letters). Students need help in the later grades to become aware of the similarities and differences in phonics, syllabication, word roots, and syntax between English and Spanish to help in their transition.

In English as a second language classes or sheltered English classes, students can learn to decode in about the same time as English-speaking children (maybe lagging a month or two) because even limited oral vocabularies are enough to teach the alphabetic principles using simple words such as *cow* or *horse*. In this, they are much like children who come from extremely low socioeconomic conditions who many times have limited oral vocabularies but are taught to read in first grade by teachers using the practices described here. One added component is necessary: teachers must ascertain that the child knows the meaning of the word being decoded.

Bibliography

Adams, M. J. 1990. *Beginning to read: Thinking and learning about print.* Cambridge, Mass.: MIT Press.

Adams, M. J., and M. Bruck, M. 1995. Resolving the "Great Debate." *American Educator* 19, no. 7: 10–20.

Adams, M. J., R. Treiman, and M. Pressley. In press. Reading, writing, and literacy. In I. Sigel and A. Renninger, eds., *Handbook of child psychology.* Volume 4: *Child psychology in practice.* New York: Wiley.

Anderson, R. C. 1992. *Research foundations for wide reading.* Commissioned by the World Bank. Urbana, Ill.: Center for the Study of Reading.

Anderson, R. C., and W. E. Nagy. 1992. The vocabulary conundrum. *American Educator* 17: 14.

Bear, D. R., M. Invernizzi, S. Templeton, and R. Johnston. 1996. *Words their way: Word study for phonics, vocabulary, and spelling.* Englewood Cliffs, N.J.: Prentice Hall.

Beck, I., and C. Juel. 1995. The role of decoding in learning to read. *American Educator* 19, no. 8: 21.

Calfee, R. C. 1995. A behind-the-scenes look at reading acquisition. *Issues in Education* 1: 77–82.

Ehri, L. C. 1994. Development of the ability to read word. In R. Ruddell and H. Singer, eds., *Theoretical models and processes of reading.* 4th ed. Newark, Del.: International Reading Association, pp. 323–58.

Foorman, B., D. Francis, T. Beeler, D. Winikates, and J. Fletcher. 1997. Early interventions for children with reading problems: Study designs and preliminary findings. *Learning Disabilities: A Multidisciplinary Journal* 8: 63–71.

Gaskins, I. W., L. C. Ehri, C. Cress, C. O'Hara, and K. Donnelly. 1997. Procedures for word learning: Making discoveries about words. *The Reading Teacher* 50, no. 4: 312–327.

Gaskins, I. W., L. C. Ehri, C. Cress, C. O'Hara, and K. Donnelly. 1997. Analyzing words and making discoveries about the alphabetic system: Activities for beginning readers. *Language Arts* 74 (March): 172–83.

Grossen, B. 1997. *Thirty years of research: What we now know about how children learn to read.* Santa Cruz, Calif.: Center for the Future of Teaching and Learning. Available on the web at: http://www.ksagroup.com/thecenter/.

Henry, M. 1990. *Words: Integrated decoding and spelling instruction based on word origin and word structure.* Austin, Tex.: Pro-Ed.

Hiebert, E. H., and B. M. Taylor, eds. 1994. *Getting reading right from the start: Effective early literacy intervention.* Boston: Allyn and Bacon.

Honig, B. 1996. *Teaching our children to read: The role of skills in a comprehensive reading program.* Thousand Oaks, Calif.: Corwin Press.

Juel, C. 1994. *Learning to read and write in one elementary school.* New York: Springer-Verlag.

Kameenui, E. J. 1996. Shakespeare and beginning reading: "Readiness is all." *Teaching Exceptional Children*, winter.

McPike, E. 1995. Learning to read: Schooling's first mission. *American Educator* 19 (spring): 12–15.

Moats, L. C. 1995. *Spelling: Development, diasability and instruction.* Baltimore: York Press.

Morgan, J. M., and D. Willows. 1997. Reducing the risk: An earlier literacy program for ESL students. Paper presented at the American Education Research Association annual meeting, Ontario Institute for Studies in Education, University of Toronto.

Morris, D. 1993. The relationship between children's concept of word in text and phoneme awareness in learning to read: A longitudinal study. *Research in the Teaching of English* 27, no. 2 (May).

Nagy, W. E. 1988. *Teaching vocabulary to improve reading comprehension.* Newark, Del.: International Reading Asssociation.

Nagy, W. E. 1995. What do we know about vocabulary? Paper presented at American Education Research Association, San Francisco, April.

Perfetti, C. A. 1995. Cognitive research can inform reading. *Education Journal of Research in Reading* 18, no. 2:106–15.

Share, D. L. 1995. Phonological recoding and self-teaching: Sine qua non of reading acquisition. *Cognition: International Journal of Cognitive Science* 55: 151–218.

Share, D. L., and K. E. Stanovich. 1995. Accommodating individual differences in critiques: Replies to our commentators. *Issues in Education: Contributions from Educational Psychology* 1: 195–221.

Share, D. L, and K. E. Stanovich. 1995. Cognitive processes in early reading development: Accommodating individual differences into a mode of acquisition. *Issues in Education: Contributions from Educational Psychology* 1: 1–57.

Shaywitz, S. E. 1996. Dyslexia. *Scientific American* 275, no. 5: 98–104

Shefelbine, J. 1995. Learning and using phonics in beginning reading. In *Scholastic literacy research papers*. New York: Scholastic.

Snider, V. 1995. A primer on phonemic awareness: What it is, why it's important, and how to teach it. *School Psychology Review* 24, no. 3: 443–55.

Stahl, S. A. Saying the "P" word: Nine guidelines for exemplary phonic instruction. *The Reading Teacher* 45 (8 April).

Stanovich, K. E. 1994. Romance and reality. *The Reading Teacher* 47, no. 4: 280–81.

Stanovich, K., and P. Stanovich. 1995. How research might inform the debate about early reading acquisition. *Journal of Research in Reading* 18, no. 2: 87–105.

Taylor, B. 1996. Looking beyond ourselves to help all children learn to read. In M. F. Graves, P. Van den Broek, and B. M. Taylor, eds., *The first R: Every child's right to read.* New York: Teachers College Press, pp. 62–69.

Torgesen, J. K. 1995. Instruction for reading disabled children: Questions about knowledge into practice. *Issues in Education: Contributions from Educational Psychology* 1: 91–95.

Torgesen, J. K., and Hecht, S. A. 1996. Preventing and remediating reading disabilities: Instructional variables that make a difference for special students. In M. F. Graves, P. Van den Broek, and B. M. Taylor, eds., *The first R; Every child's right to read.* New York; Teachers College Press, pp. 133–59.

Torgensen, J. K., R. Wagner, C. A. Rashotte, A. W. Alexander, and T. Conway. 1997. Preventive and remedial intervention for children with severe reading disabilities. *Learning Disabilities: A Multidisciplinary Journal* 8: 51–62.

Tunmer, W. E., and J. W. Chapman. 1996. Beginning readers' self-reports on strategies used for identifying unfamiliar words in text. Paper presented at the annual meeting of the New Zealand Association for Research in Education, Massey University.

Vellutino, F. R. 1991. Introduction to three studies on reading acquisition: Convergent findings on theoretic foundation of code-oriented versus whole-language approachhes to reading instruction. *Journal of Educational Psychology* 83, no. 4: 437–43.

Williams, J. P. 1991. The meaning of a phonics base for reading instruction. In *All language and the creation of literacy.* Proceedings of the Orton Dyslexia Society Symposia "Whole Language and Phonics and Literacy and Language." Baltimore, Md.: Orton Dyslexia Society, pp. 9–19.

Louisa Cook Moats

Spelling and Language Structure: An Essential Foundation for Literacy

Evidence abounds that many children are completing school with insufficient mastery of spoken and written language, including reading and spelling. In California, 59 percent of fourth graders scored "below basic"[1] on the 1994 National Assessment of Educational Progress, a figure that tied California for last place nationally and that registered a decline from 1992. In other states children might do better, but they are not doing well. In 1995, at all grade levels, Illinois schoolchildren's scores on the state assessment in reading reached their lowest level since the testing program began in 1988. In the spring of 1997, 41 percent of Minnesota's eighth graders flunked a basic reading test. The governor's office in Texas has worked actively over the past several years to reverse a downward trend in language arts education that is most apparent in city schools with poor and bilingual populations. Even Congress is developing initiatives to improve teacher preparation and classroom practice in reading because of nationwide expressions of concern.

1. According to the NAEP definitions, this level identifies little or no mastery of knowledge or skills necessary to perform work at each grade level. (U.S. Department of Education, National Center for Education Statistics, National Assessment Governing Board, *Reading Framework for the 1994 National Assessment of Educational Progress*, 1994.)

Why the trend? Many factors have contributed, but among them must be the curriculum materials and textbooks used in teacher preparation, which have included less and less information about our language. Textbooks for teachers and instructional materials for children are light on concepts that once constituted daily classroom fare. In California, spelling, grammar, and phonics programs were banished in the 1987 textbook adoption; consequently, teachers for ten years have worked with little guidance from publishers about how to teach the structure of words, sentences, paragraphs, or essays. In the name of meaning-emphasis instruction, many classrooms have been exclusively focused on the message of print and oblivious to the importance of its form. An essential aspect of language study has been neglected, with unfortunate consequences. Although meaning making is the obvious goal of reading and writing, communication of meaning and manipulation of form are inextricable complements deserving equal emphasis in instruction.

Within this framework, three points bear elaboration: (a) good readers and spellers have a better understanding of language structure than poor readers and spellers; (b) language form, as in spelling or sentence structure, is intrinsically interesting and can make sense; and (c) teaching the structure of the language at the sound, symbol, and word level enhances comprehension and composition. In the interest of space, the spelling system will be the focus of this chapter, but similar arguments can be made for knowledge of word meanings (vocabulary), sentence structure, and text organization.

Apprehending Language Structure

Spelling difficulties are common among individuals with language or attentional weaknesses and are always found in individuals with dyslexia or specific reading disabilities (Lyon

1995). Learning to spell is more challenging than learning to read and can be difficult even for students who are bright and motivated. The ability to remember the exact letter sequence in words is minimally correlated with other kinds of intelligence or even language comprehension. Spelling difficulty is caused by insensitivity to language structure, particularly at the level of speech sound awareness, and by weaknesses in a specific memory system that is responsible for recalling letter sequences. This specific orthographic memory system is not related to the kind of visual memory that is involved in nonlinguistic, visual-spatial reasoning such as that needed for recall of a design, a map, a face, or a place. Because these functions are independent, it is not possible to improve spelling ability by drilling a student on "visual memory" aside from practicing words themselves.

Some people are just good spellers and seem to recall words easily from exposure to them in print. Seeing words is enough to remember them. Those good spellers usually attend to speech sounds easily, demonstrate sensitivity to language structure at other levels such as morphology, are good at reading unfamiliar words by sounding them out, and are more able to learn linguistic complexities than individuals who spell poorly (Bailet 1990; Carlisle 1987; Liberman, Rubin, Duques, and Carlisle 1985; Shankweiler, Lundquist, Dreyer, and Dickinson 1996). Conversely, those who spell poorly, even if they read well, usually demonstrate at least subtle difficulties with other aspects of language, especially the ability to notice language structure (sounds, syllables, orthographic patterns, and meaningful word parts) while remembering words. Most average students cluster between these extremes; they can learn patterns if they are taught but do not necessarily learn them because they are exposed to words in print. Thus it is important to emphasize, through organized lists and explicit instruction, what is regular and systematic about the spelling system.

The ability to spell is influenced by genetics, and it is true in part that "good spellers are born but not made." The underlying inherited trait that affects both word reading and spelling is language awareness, a metalinguistic ability that determines how well an individual can manipulate language at the phonological and morphological levels (Pennington 1995). Even with poor spellers, however, early and well-designed instruction that highlights the structure of language and that gives sufficient practice using word patterns can make a substantial difference in spelling achievement (Moats 1996). Effective teaching requires knowledge of English orthography and its relation to sound.

English Orthographic Structure

The structure of written English reflects historical influences, orthographic patterns invented by scribes, and the intrinsic properties of spoken language itself. Within the class of alphabetic writing systems, English is the most complex and variant. Our spelling system is characterized as a deep or morphographemic orthography by linguists because English uses symbols and symbol clusters to spell sounds, syllables, and meaningful parts of words (see figure 1). It is not a straightforward, phonetic transcription of speech. Historical changes in the dominant culture and politics of England account for much of the complexity and variation of English spelling.

HISTORICAL INFLUENCES

Anglo-Saxon and Its Roots. The most common, frequent words of English are preserved from its oldest layer, Anglo-Saxon or Old English. Anglo-Saxon, in turn, evolved from a primitive Indo-European tongue (for historical sources on the evolution of English, see Balmuth 1992; Bryson 1990; Fromkin and Rodman 1993; McCrum, Cran, and McNeil 1986). Similarities in the vocabulary, grammatical patterns, and phonological features of all the Indo-European languages attest to their com-

WRITING SYSTEMS

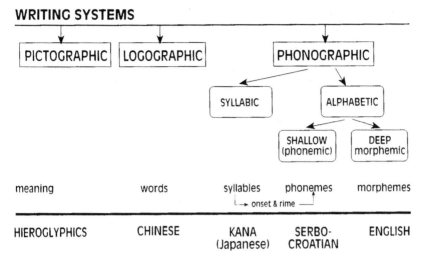

Figure 1. Writing Systems. From P. H. K. Seymour, "Cognitive Theories of Spelling and Implications for Education," in C. Sterling and C. Robson, eds., *Psychology, Spelling, and Education* (Clevedon, U.K.: Multilingual Matters Ltd., 1992), p. 53.

mon origin. Words for animals, family members, numbers, emotions, and universal daily activities tend to be similar across related language groups that evolved from the same ancestral language.

The proto-Germanic language from which Anglo-Saxon developed was spoken in a territory around Denmark somewhat before the Christian era. Words in modern English believed to have come from proto-Germanic include *rain, drink,* and *broad.* The language was highly inflected and included derived forms similar to our present-day *heal-health, hold-held, sell-sold, bake-baked,* where the past tense involves a vowel shift and an ending with the tongue behind or between the teeth. *Ride-rode, stand-stood, choose-chose* are proto-Germanic descendants in which a vowel shift was maintained in the past tense verb form after a final inflection was dropped. Proto-Germanic words were always stressed on the first syllable with the exception of compound verbs such as *abide* and *begin.*

Anglo-Saxon, the German family ancestor of modern English, gave us words for work (*shepherd, plough, work*), for numbers (*one, hundred*), for body parts (*heart, knee, foot*), for basic sentiments (*love, hate, laughter*), and for animals (*sheep, goat, horse*). Of the hundred most often used words in English, all can be traced to Anglo-Saxon origins. Our grammatical glue words or function words are almost uniformly Anglo-Saxon (*the, a, and, you, to, would*). They are often one-syllable words. In Anglo-Saxon or Old English, compound forms were stressed on the first syllable, as in *grandmother*. Because of vowel shift patterns and inflection changes that occurred as Old English became Middle English and then Modern English, spoken and written forms such as *foot-feet, tooth-teeth, goose-geese, climb, told*, and *find* evolved and took root.

From the Anglo-Saxon layer of language came most of our consonant and vowel correspondences; only a few additional phonic correspondences were adopted from Greek spelling patterns (y for /I/ as in *gym*, ph for /f/ as in *philosophy*; and ch for /k/ as in *chorus*) and no new correspondences were contributed by Latin. However, as modern English adopted words from many other languages, spellings from those languages were often assimilated as well (*barbecue, plaza, marijuana*, and *chocolate* from Spanish; *bayou, butte, levee*, and *picayune* from French; *pizza* and *cello* from Italian).

The Anglo-Saxon layer of English, then, accounts for most of our irregular spellings; the irregular spellings are among our most commonly used words and often have endured centuries of pronunciation shift. Beyond the basic vocabulary, spelling becomes much more predictable or pattern based.

The Latin Layer of English. The Latin-based vocabulary incorporated into Anglo-Saxon after the Norman invasion of Britain in 1066 was the language of scholars, nobles, and those of high social class. The Normans, led by William the Conqueror, were a French-speaking people whose cultured men of letters wrote in French and Latin, languages that were closely related members of an Indo-European family. These languages contributed thousands of words such as *amorous, malevolent, fortitude, maternal,* and *residence* to English that were often used in the language of text and scholarship. After the monarchies of France and England officially separated in the thirteenth and fourteenth centuries, the upswing in patriotic sentiment in England led to a new embrace of Middle English by the upper classes, who hitherto had regarded English as the crude language of the masses. English, for more than two centuries the language of the uneducated, had been adopted by all Britons by the beginning of the fourteenth century. Shortly thereafter, the first great works of English literature were written, including those of Geoffrey Chaucer, and, by the early fifteenth century, during the reign of Henry V, English had become the official language for written communication. Close to modern English, this amalgam of Anglo-Saxon, Latin, and French had undergone rapid evolution and several major pronunciation shifts.

The Greek Influence. The Italian Renaissance reached England in the mid–sixteenth century, bringing with it a renewed cultural interest in classical Roman and Greek language, art, and literature. The Greek influence on English can be traced to the residence of Saint Augustine in Canterbury during the tenth century; he used words such as *disciple, apostle,* and *psalm,* religious terms with Greek roots. Contact with Greek culture had been maintained by followers of the Greek Orthodox religion, who entered into commercial and cultural exchanges with the Italians in the fourteenth and fifteenth centuries and began exporting Greek vocabulary, scholarship, and aesthetics. The scholars who migrated west from Constantinople stimulated interest in the study of language, an academic discipline that had flourished in ancient Greece. Tudor scholars in the mid–sixteenth century deliberately borrowed words from the classical vocabulary to embellish and elevate their prose. Words such as *catastrophe, lexicon, atmosphere, pneumonia, skeleton, gravity, encyclopedia,* and *psychology,* of Greek origin, became English words in this way.

The layers of language in English orthography are represented in Henry's (1988) schematic diagram of sound, syllable, and morpheme structures by language of origin (see figure 2). This model can serve as a general organizational scheme for a word study curriculum spanning all eight elementary grades, with the emphasis shifting from Anglo-Saxon to Latin-based morphemes around the beginning of fourth grade.

SOUND-SYMBOL CORRESPONDENCES IN AMERICAN ENGLISH: HOW THEY WORK

The Roman alphabet is insufficient for English spelling: the twenty-six letters are too few to represent the forty-plus phonemes of English.[2] Letter combinations are thus necessary to spell some consonants (such as *th, wh, sh, ch, ng*) and many of the fifteen vowels (*oo, ee, i-e,* and so forth). Graphemes, or the letter(s) that correspond to speech sounds, include the *eigh* in *weight,* the *ough* in *though,* and the *tch* in *batch.* The letter combinations *ea, ei, ie, ee, ey,* and *e-e* are all used for long *e* (/i/ in the international phonetic alphabet). Although many graphemes have silent letters, the letter groups form stable, predictable configurations that correspond to speech sounds, and most silent letters belong to stable configurations used in discrete sets of words. They are an indispensable part of the grapheme unit.

More than 250 graphemes are used to spell the forty phonemes of English. Reading is thus a convergent process whereby

---

2. Standard linguistics texts do not agree on the number or features of English phonemes; but most include at least forty, and some include as many as fifty-two.

	Sound	Syllable	Morpheme
Anglo-Saxon	Consonants • single • blends • digrpahs Vowels • short/long *r* controlled • teams • diphthongs	Six types • closed • open • *r* controlled • *c-le* • vowel team • *vce*	Compounds Inflections
Romance (Latin)			Prefixes Suffixes Roots Plurals
Greek	*y* = /I/ *ch* = /K/ • chorus *ph* = /f/ • sphynx		Combining forms (scientific vocabulary) (micro + meter) (psych + ology) Plurals • crises

Figure 2. Language Curriculum (after Marcia Henry, *Words*, Pro-Ed, 1996).

a limited set of sounds is mapped onto various ways of spelling them. Spelling, by contrast, is a divergent symbolic activity because several spellings for the same sound and the patterns in which those spellings are used must be learned. The units of spelling from which words are constructed include single consonants, consonant digraphs, consonant blend spellings, and silent-letter consonant spellings. Vowel spelling patterns, including single-letter spellings, vowel teams, long-vowel consonant *e*, and vowel *r* spellings are part of the basic set of Anglo-Saxon spelling conventions. These can be mapped onto the intrinsic organization of the vowel sound system, which is an articulatory progression from front to back and from high to low (see figure 3).

Predictability in English Spelling. English sound-symbol correspondences are not as capricious or unpredictable as critics

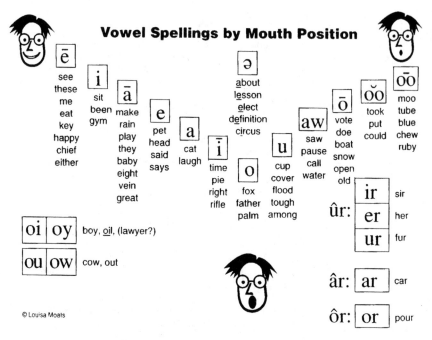

Figure 3.   Vowel Spellings by Mouth Position

assert. Rather, the correspondence system used to spell the individual speech sounds is about 85 percent predictable if the position of sounds and the sounds that precede or follow a target sound are taken into account (Hanna, Hanna, Hodges, and Rudorf 1966; Venezky 1970). The sound /f/ cannot be spelled with a *gh* at the beginning of a syllable but can be at the end, as in *rough* (although *ff* is the preferred spelling for /f/ at the ends of words with a short vowel preceding the /f/). Meaning and morphological structure determine spelling: *played* would not be spelled *plade*. The sounds that come before or after a given sound also contribute to the patterns; for example, the /f/ in *sphere* must be spelled with a *ph* because it comes after /s/. Words most recently assimilated into English tend to retain spelling from the language of origin, such as *charade* from French, *spaghetti* from

Italian, and *mosquito* from Spanish. The system is variant because, even within these constraints, there are "choice" spellings, different ways to spell the same sound. The most notorious variable in English is probably the phoneme /sh/, as in *sherry, sugar, mission, conscious, special, chef,* and *objection,* although in many cases the ambiguity in spelling this sound can be reduced by knowing the word's origin and meaning (*sh* is the most common spelling, but many borrowed words from French preserve the *ch* spelling for /sh/, as in *Charlotte, chagrin,* and *Cher*).

Facts about English Spelling

- Fifty percent of English words are spelled accurately by sound-symbol correspondence rules alone

- Thirty-seven percent more are spelled with only one error

- Ten percent more are spelled accurately if word meaning, origin, and morphology are considered

- About 2 percent are true oddities[3]

Predictability is not a dichotomous characteristic, an either/ or feature of spelling in English, and materials or tests that classify words this way are oversimplifying linguistic reality. The psychological or cognitive factors that enable people to remember words include the intensity of emotional associations with a word (*sex*), its frequency in an individual's writing, whether it follows a pattern at all, and whether it is so unusual that its oddity makes it memorable (*ski*). In addition, some spellings are less probable in the overall rule system but are members of a small family of common words that are just as easily learned as words that conform to a domain-inclusive rule. For example, *he,*

---

3. These estimates are based on the computerized analysis of English conducted in 1966 by Hanna, Hanna, Hodges, and Rudorf.

she, be, and *we* all share the spelling for long *e* and are among the most common words in the language, even though they violate the rule for spelling at the ends of words (*ee* is more often used, as in *bee, fee, glee, thee, tree, free, knee, agree, tee, flee, scree*). If we construct a predictability scale that represents a continuum of absolutely predictable spellings to spellings that recur as part of a family but are less common than the alternative graphemes for the same sound, it might look like this:

0	1	2	3	4	5
tin	quit	care	catch	pie	hurt
pup	beck	hope	dodge	tea	weigh
bad	crab	kite	child	put	feud

0 = no other way to spell the sounds
5 = low-frequency choice, still in a word "family"

To become aware of the kind of orthographic pattern perception that underlies the successful learning of English spelling, consider the following spellings for the sound /k/. They are variable but constrained by the sounds and letters surrounding the /k/ phoneme.

counter	kickball	stack	question
cattle	ketchup	mock	queen
cup	keep	fleck	quit
comb	kind	bucket	quandary

At the end of a syllable following a short vowel, *ck* is the preferred spelling for /k/ (*decks, sticker, bucket*). The *qu* combination, which represents /kw/, always occurs at the beginnings of syllables. Whether the letter *k* or *c* is used to spell /k/ at the beginnings of syllables depends on the letter or phoneme that follows it. When /k/ is followed by vowels spelled with *a, o,* or *u,* the letter *c* is used (*cat, cushion, cozy*); when /k/ is followed by vowel letters *i* or *e*, the letter *k* is used, as in *kite, ketchup, keen*. In consonant blends, /k/ followed by /r/ or /l/ is always spelled with a *c* (*clean, crazy*). To add one more layer of complexity, word origin also determines spelling: *ch* for /k/ is used almost exclusively in words of Greek origin such as *chorus* and *orchestra*.

Most people never memorize such patterns and are not consciously aware of them until they are asked to spell a nonsense word such as *kem, shlock,* or *cluzz* and explain why they chose a letter for the sound. However, good spellers have internalized such patterns from exposure to many examples, and good spellers notice the details of orthographic structure at several layers of language organization. Effective instruction will exploit the inherent organization of print, make it explicit and engaging for students, and connect it to word meaning and word choice in composition.

Teaching the Structure of Language

To learn to read and spell, children must be at least tacitly aware of the phonemes in words (Ball and Blachman 1991; Tangel and Blachman 1992, 1995; Treiman 1993). Evidence is substantial that early reading and spelling difficulty is marked by deficits in phoneme awareness tasks and other skills dependent on phonemic processing (Liberman et al. 1985; Lyon 1995; Vellutino, Scanlon, and Tanzman 1994). Poor readers consistently have greater difficulty than good readers on tests of phoneme awareness (how many speech sounds are in *toast?*), phoneme segmentation (can you say *meat* without the /m/?), rhyming (what rhymes with *stone?*), fluency and accuracy of spoken word production, and nonsense word reading tasks. Poor spellers also do more poorly than good spellers on tests of word pronunciation, short-term memory for lists and nonsense words, speed of symbol copying, and often mental computation. As with reading, when children are taught explicitly to identify the speech sounds in words, using exercises such as placing the sounds on their fingers or marking them with chips, their spelling improves (Adams 1990; Tangel and Blachman 1992, 1995). Especially in the beginning stages, spelling develops in accordance with one's ability to specify the phonemes in words. When children can spell phonetically, usually at about mid-first-grade level, they are ready to learn standard spellings. Phonological skill supports memory for orthographic sequences (Foorman et al. 1991).

Orthographic patterns should be taught in an organized sequence that respects the progression in which word knowledge develops (Templeton and Bear 1992). Vowel and consonant correspondences within words are learned before the patterns of syllable connection, and syllable patterns are learned before morphological structures. Within each stage, certain phonological features and spelling patterns are more difficult than others and require more care in instruction. At all stages of development, vowel spellings cause more errors than consonant spellings (Schlagal 1992). Short vowels are challenging for children to identify, differentiate, and associate with symbols because of the similarities in articulation (Ehri 1987). Long vowel spellings have confusable letter patterns. Vowel spellings are not mastered by most children until fourth grade (Schlagal 1992). Thus, our programs should teach vowels with care. A chart that teaches the identity of vowel phonemes, their articulation, and their common spellings (see figure 3) can enlighten children who do not remember words simply by viewing them in context.

According to Schlagal (1992) and Treiman (1993), the consonant phonemes also vary in difficulty. Nasal phonemes (/n/, /m/, /ng/) before consonants and after vowels (as in *point*, *camp*, and *stink*) tend to get lost in the early spellings of younger children. Thus they will write *jup* for *jump* and *wet* for *went* until they develop awareness of the nasal consonant present in the words.

Consonant blends are much harder for normally progressing children than single consonants (Treiman 1993) and are mastered later. Omission of the sounds /l/, /r/, /m/, /n/, and /ng/ from consonant blends accounts for a significant proportion of errors through sixth grade. Many children need to practice comparing words, such as *cash, crash,* and *clash* or *flesh* and *fresh,* until they become aware of the subtle differences among them. In all grades up to sixth and probably beyond, *r*-controlled vowels (*girl, turn*), consonant doubling (*pebble, sunny*), and recall of vowel markers (as in *gait* and *gate, feat* and *feet*) are relatively more difficult than other correspondences. To learn, they will require more practice and conscious attention than some other types of words.

The ability to judge what sounds, syllables, and morphemes compose words is an important aspect of teaching spelling to children who experience difficulty remembering. Techniques such as saying syllables slowly and asking the child to put a sound on each finger can be helpful, especially if a teacher can give corrective feedback for omissions or substitutions of sounds. It is always desirable to ensure that a student can pronounce a word, read a word, divide the syllables or morphemes, and define a word before trying to memorize its spelling. Effective word study involves taking words apart, putting pieces together, underlining key elements, and discussing how the word is structured, as well as writing the word many times.

Through sixth grade and beyond, many common spelling errors occur on words having suffixes that change the spelling of a base word, especially those that involve the doubling rule (*referred*) and the silent-*e* rule (*writing*) (Moats 1996; Schlagal 1992). Many errors occur on the monosyllabic past tense (-*ed* pronounced as /t/ or /d/, as in *attached* and *enjoyed*) and on ambiguous consonants such as /k/, which have several possible spellings. The spelling of unstressed schwa, /ə/, especially in longer words of Latin origin, becomes an increasingly important source of error as children learn longer words in third grade and up. Errors commonly occur on indistinct syllables such as the *i* in *president* and the *e* in *competition*. Such ambiguities can be resolved for students by ensuring their understanding of morphology: that *president* is related to *preside* and *compete* is related to *competition*. When a spelling word list is introduced, students benefit from saying words slowly, talking about their meaning, connecting them to words of similar origin and spelling pattern, deconstructing syllables and morphemes, and then using the words as often as possible in context.

Fluent writing is facilitated by automatic recall of word form. Beyond the recognition of word structure, many children need a great deal of practice to establish word habits. Dictation of appealing language, proofreading exercises, and novel activities such as typing on the computer or writing on the chalkboard are all helpful in building spelling proficiency. Some odd words (*one, of, does, who, you*) are best learned through multisensory tracing routines.

Summary

Learning to spell entails appreciation of word form, its connection to word meaning, and its application to writing. What is often treated as a rote or insignificant skill can be lively, interesting, and enjoyable. Appreciation of words in turn engenders appreciation of language. Word knowledge is associated with better comprehension and composition, not the inhibition of reading and writing as some have claimed.

Discovery of orthography should begin with attention to subtle differences in the sounds of words. Speech sound awareness facilitates both reading and spelling. Those with severe spelling and reading problems often require careful attention to the development of phonological skill before they can achieve success with print. As sound-letter relationships are taught, children can be led to appreciate the origin and structure of our alphabetic writing system. Systematic study of word patterns at increasingly complex levels of language organization should reflect the order inherent in the writing system itself as well as the typical progression of children's learning.

Skillful instruction of spelling and other language skills requires content knowledge on the part of the teacher in addition to a repertoire of instructional methods. Surveys of teachers' knowledge of phonology, morphology, and orthographic structure (Moats 1995) reveal that most teachers, even experienced teachers, possess only the most superficial acquaintance with their own language. Superficial knowledge, in turn, is inadequate for sequencing instruction, explaining and choosing examples of concepts, or giving corrective feedback after students make mistakes. This observation is not intended to criticize teachers for what they do not know but to point to the necessity for teaching them the information. Most teachers, when taught the basics of phonology, orthography, morphology, and other dimensions of language, are grateful for the insight that such content allows and wonder why they were never asked to learn it. Those who develop linguistic understanding usually endorse its importance. Knowledge of language, especially knowledge of orthography, enables teachers to impart with delight the history, form, and meaning of words, even as they teach composition. If teachers believe that learning to spell is learning about words from many interesting angles, children will become believers as well.

References

Adams, M. J. 1990. *Beginning to Read: Thinking and Learning about Print.* Cambridge, Mass.: MIT Press.

Bailet, L. 1990. "Spelling Rule Usage among Students with Learning Disabilities and Normally Achieving Students." *Journal of Learning Disabilities* 23: 121–28.

Ball, A., and B. Blachman. 1991. "Does Phoneme Segmentation Training in Kindergarten Make a Difference in Early Word Recognition and Developmental Spelling?" *Reading Research Quarterly* 26: 49–66.

Balmuth, M. 1992. *The Roots of Phonics: A Historical Introduction.* Baltimore, Md.: York Press.

Bryson, B. 1990. *The Mother Tongue: English and How It Got That Way.* New York: Avon Books.

Carlisle, J. F. 1987. "The Use of Morphological Knowledge in Spelling Derived Forms by Learning Disabled and Normal Students." *Annals of Dyslexia* 37: 90–108.

Ehri, L. 1987. "Learning to Read and Spell Words." *Journal of Reading Behavior* 19: 5–31.

Foorman, B., D. V. Navoy, D. J. Francis, and D. Liberman. 1991. "How Letter-Sound Instruction Mediates Progress in First-Grade Reading and Spelling." *Journal of Educational Psychology* 83: 456–59.

Fromkin, V., and R. Rodman. 1993. *An Introduction to Language.* Fort Worth, Tex.: Harcourt Brace Jovanovich.

Hanna, P. R., J. S. Hanna, R. E. Hodges, and E. H. Rudorf. 1966. *Phoneme-Grapheme Correspondences as Cues to Spelling Improvement.* Washington, D.C.: U.S. Government Printing Office.

Henry, M. 1988. "Beyond Phonics: Integrated Decoding and Spelling Instruction Based on Word Origin and Structure." *Annals of Dyslexia* 38: 258–75.

Liberman, I. Y., H. Rubin, S. Duques, and J. Carlisle. 1985. "Linguistic Abilities and Spelling Proficiency in Kindergarteners and Adult Poor Spellers." In D. B. Gray and J. F. Kavanagh, eds., *Orthography, Reading, and Dyslexia.* Parkton, Md.: York Press, pp. 137–53.

Lyon, G. R. 1995. "Research Initiatives and Discoveries in Learning Disabilities." *Journal of Child Neurology* 10: 120–26.

McCrum, R., W. Cran, and R. McNeil. 1986. *The Story of English.* New York: Viking.

Moats, L. C. 1994. "Knowledge of the Structure of Spoken and Written Language: The Missing Foundation in Teacher Education." *Annals of Dyslexia* 44: 81–102.

————. 1995. *Spelling: Development, Disability, and Instruction.* Baltimore, Md.: York Press.

————. 1996. "Phonological Spelling Errors in the Writing of Dyslexic Adolescents." *Reading and Writing: An Interdisciplinary Journal* 8: 105–19.

Pennington, B. 1995. "Genetics of Learning Disabilities." *Journal of Child Neurology* 10: S69–S77.

Read, C. 1986. *Children's Creative Spelling.* Boston: Routledge and Kegan Paul.

Rubin, H., and N. Eberhardt. 1996. "Facilitating Invented Spelling through Language Analysis Instruction: An Integrated Model." *Reading and Writing: An Interdisciplinary Journal* 8: 27–43.

Rubin, H., P. A. Patterson, and N. Kantor. 1991. "Morphological Development and Writing Ability in Children and Adults." *Language, Speech, and Hearing Services in the Schools* 22: 228–35.

Schlagal, R. 1992. "Patterns of Orthographic Development in the Middle Grades." In S. Templeton and D. Bear, eds., *Development of Orthographic Knowledge and the Foundations of Literacy: A Memorial Festschrift for Edmund H. Henderson.* Hillsdale, N.J.: Lawrence Erlbaum, pp. 31–52.

Shankweiler, D., E. Lundquist, L. G. Dreyer, and C. C. Dickinson. 1996. "Reading and Spelling Difficulties in High School Students: Causes and Consequences." *Reading and Writing: An Interdisciplinary Journal* 8: 267–94.

Tangel, D. M., and B. A. Blachman. 1992. "Effect of Phoneme Awareness Instruction on Kindergarten Children's Invented Spelling." *Journal of Reading Behavior* 24: 233–61.

————. 1995. "Effect of Phoneme Awareness Instruction on the Invented Spelling of First Grade Children: A One Year Follow-Up." *Journal of Reading Behavior* 27: 153–85.

Templeton, S., and D. B. Bear. 1992. *Development of Orthographic Knowledge and the Foundations of Literacy: A Memorial Festschrift for Edmund H. Henderson.* Hillsdale, N.J.: Lawrence Erlbaum.

Treiman, R. T. 1993. *Beginning to Spell.* New York: Oxford University Press.

Vellutino, F. R., D. M. Scanlon, and M. S. Tanzman. 1994. "Components of Reading Ability: Issues and Problems in Operationalizing Word Identification, Phonological Coding, and Orthographic Coding." In

Frames of Reference for the Assessment of Learning Disabilities: New Views on Measurement Issues, ed. G. R. Lyon. Baltimore, Md.: Paul Brookes, pp. 279–32.

Venezky, R. L. 1970. *The Structure of English Orthography.* The Hague: Mouton.

Harold W. Stevenson

Mathematics Achievement: First in the World by the Year 2000?

$\mathbf{A}$ set of national goals that would guide educational progress through the 1990s was adopted by the fifty governors of the United States at a meeting in Charlottesville, Virginia, in 1989. The governors were joined by President George Bush, and later the goals were slightly expanded under the leadership of President Bill Clinton. Goals 2000, as the program became known, dealt with the preparation of children for school, citizenship, high school completion, adult literacy, teacher education, parental participation, and safe schools. The goal we are interested in here is the one proposing that, "by the year 2000, United States students will be first in the world in mathematics and science achievement."

The question immediately arises as to whether this goal is realistic, for indications before 1989 were that, rather than being world leaders, U.S. students were particularly weak in mathematics and science. For example, the Second International Mathematics Study of the early 1980s, which reported scores on mathematics tests of eighth-grade students from twenty different countries and of twelfth-grade students from fifteen countries, showed that the average scores of U.S. students were surpassed by those of students from all but a few countries (McKnight et al. 1987). In algebra, for example, the average score of the U.S. students was next to the bottom; in geometry it was lower than scores of students from all countries except Israel, Swaziland, Nigeria, and Luxembourg.

It is always possible that remarkable improvements could occur in the presence of a challenging goal. This seems unlikely in the present case, however, for results for the U.S. students from the Third International Mathematics and Science Study (TIMSS) conducted in the mid-1990s (Peak 1996; Peak 1997) are as discouraging as those found earlier. With only three years to go until the year 2000, there seems no likelihood that U.S. students will climb to first place by the end of this century. The TIMSS data reveal little indication of improvement in the status of the U.S. students in comparison with that of the students from the forty other countries that participated in this large, comprehensive study. The top scores in the mathematics tests at both grades four and eight were obtained by students from Singapore (#1), Korea (#2), Japan (#3), and Hong Kong (#4). For example, the average score of the U.S. fourth-grade students in mathematics was 545; that of the Singapore students was 625. The Singapore eighth graders—again the top scorers— had an average score of 643, and the U.S. students, 500. (Scores on the test were scaled so that 68 percent of all scores lie between 400 and 600.)

The picture is somewhat different for science at the fourth grade. The Korean students' average score of 597 was the highest received. Below Korea were six countries, including the United States, whose scores did not differ significantly from one another. However, this high level of performance by the U.S. students was not sustained. By the eighth grade, the top scorers were Singapore, Japan, and Korea; the Hong Kong students were displaced by those from the Czech Republic. Singapore students had an average score of 607, and the U.S. students, 534. Results for high school students that recently became available show that the status of U.S. students has continued to decline through the twelfth grade.

Questioning the Data

Some critics have been unwilling to accept the low scores of U.S. students as a fair assessment of the students' levels of achievement. One proposal, for example, is that U.S. students are creative problem solvers, whereas students in countries such as those of East Asia simply learn routine operations. If this is true, the superiority of East Asian students should be greatest in areas such as arithmetic, where problems can often be solved in a rote fashion, whereas the American students should be more competitive in tasks involving problem solving, such as trigonometry.

We can evaluate this criticism by analyzing the results of a test of mathematics that we administered to more than six thousand eleventh-grade students in six different locations. This study is part of a long-term series of studies of students' achievement in mathematics that we have been conducting in East Asia, Europe, and North America. The test contained five different types of items, ranging from arithmetic to advanced mathematics (see figure 1). Two trends are apparent: first, there is a marked decline in performance in all six countries as the problems become more difficult, and, second, the superiority of East Asian students is apparent in all areas of mathematics.

Another frequent comment about comparative studies of academic achievement is that the U.S. population is heterogeneous; consequently, an average is not a good representation of what students are capable of doing. Average scores are low, it is argued, because the distribution of scores is pulled down by the poor performance of some groups of students. Furthermore, the argument continues, the best students in the United States are as capable as the best students in any country.

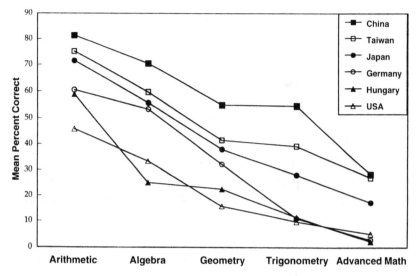

Figure 1.   Performance of Students on the Five Types of Problems in the High School Test of Mathematics

A response to these suggestions can be obtained by looking at the distributions of students' scores. Support is obtained if there is a piling up of scores at the low end of the U.S. distributions and if the top scores are comparable to the scores of the top students in other countries. The data do not support either possibility. The distributions of scores of both the U.S. students and those from other countries follow the typical normal curve but a curve that is displaced downward for the U.S. students.

There is no evidence for other charges, such as the United States includes truly representative samples of its students in comparative studies but that other countries selectively test only their better students. Other explanations, such as the proposal that U.S. students are not as intellectually capable as East Asian students, have no support in the research literature. The suggestion that the longer school day in East Asian schools underlies the students' superior performance does not take into account the fact that much of the additional time at school is devoted to extracurricular activities. The longer school year may offer students additional time to acquire the curriculum, but, on the basis of our observational studies, it is not the length of the year but the teachers' mastery of the content of the lessons and their remarkable teaching abilities that distinguish East Asian classroom practices from those of their Western counterparts. We must conclude, therefore, that U.S. elementary and secondary school students are not competitive with their peers in some East Asian and European countries in mathematics and science and that there is little likelihood that U.S. students will attain the goal proposed in Goals 2000 of being number one in the world in mathematics and science achievement. What we need now are some more convincing explanations of the differences in academic achievement. One of the first places for exploration is the classroom.

Classroom Observations

Two types of observation are commonly conducted in classrooms. In the first, narrative records are made of everything that occurred during a lesson. The records are then coded according to the presence or absence of certain behaviors of interest. From these coded data, frequencies of occurrence of particular kinds of behavior can be determined. A second, time-sampling type of observation requires the observer to follow a predetermined schedule of observation and to note on a coding sheet whether certain types of behavior occurred. More recently, a third observational method has been introduced in TIMSS. Television cameras record the complete lesson, and the tapes are then submitted to a computer program from which detailed descriptions of classroom activities can be obtained (Stigler 1996).

A comparison of Japanese and U.S. lessons clarifies some of the ways in which the teaching procedures differ between East

Asia and the West. We can assume, on the basis of the results of observational studies conducted with large samples of first-, fifth-, and eighth-grade classrooms, that the teaching practices are consistent within each country during these years (Lee, Graham, and Stevenson 1996; Stevenson et al. 1987; Stigler 1996). Whether this is also the case for high school lessons is unclear, for careful comparative studies of high school classes have not yet been conducted.

The Japanese Lesson

Underlying instruction in the typical Japanese classroom is the concept of a lesson. Rather than focusing on impromptu responses to students' questions or on unplanned developments during the course of the period, the lesson follows a coherent, integrated plan consisting of three stages: introduction of the problem, development of solutions, and a review of what has been learned.

Mathematics lessons often begin with problems related to meaningful events in the students' everyday lives. After the teacher is confident that the students understand the problem, she asks the students to devise their own solutions. A common directive is along these lines: "Think of as many different solutions as possible; don't worry about getting the correct answer. Just come up with as many different solutions as you can."

Because the size of classes in East Asian classrooms is large— usually from thirty-five to fifty students—and the teacher has no assistants, the most common mode of teaching is through whole-class involvement. All students know that it is likely that they will be called on either to describe their solutions or to respond to the solutions proposed by others. Students are therefore attentive both during the time they must devise their own solutions and during recitations by other members of the class. Rather than decide which are the most effective solutions, the teacher asks the students their reason for choosing one solution over another. After the class has evaluated the various solutions, the teacher presents additional problems for practice, sometimes using hands-on materials, sometimes demonstrating concepts at the chalkboard, and sometimes giving the students additional, carefully constructed work sheets. The class ends with the teacher summarizing the lesson and then providing additional practice problems to be completed during the remaining class time or at home.

Because the large East Asian classes necessarily include students of different ability levels and learning styles, the teachers follow the pattern of instruction-practice-evaluation several times during the course of a lesson. By varying the avenues of instruction, providing thought-provoking problems, and giving feedback to the students after each cycle, it is expected that all students will be able to understand the concepts being taught.

Japanese teachers follow carefully planned procedures for teaching students the concepts involved in the lesson and allocate smaller amounts of time to teaching routine mathematical operations. Here is an example:

> The Japanese teacher asks the students to take the red triangles out of their "Math Sets," colorful boxes of materials used in mathematics lessons. "Let's make designs. Use the triangles to make any design you wish."
>
> The teacher moves about the classroom, observing the children's progress. After allowing the students sufficient time, she selects three students and asks them to draw their designs on the chalkboard. "This is a boat," says the first student, pointing out how the triangles form the hull and sails of the boat. The second student describes how the triangles were used to make a butterfly. The third student has made a rectangle and points out how the two triangles fit together.
>
> The teacher stands back and looks a bit perplexed. How,

she asks, could one determine the area of one of the triangles. Hands shoot up, and one of the students explains: "We know that the area of a rectangle is the height times the base. A triangle is half that; so we take half the height times the base." The teacher asks the class if they agree and when they do, restates the problem.

One can assume that if none of the children had drawn the rectangle the teacher would have had the class use their triangles to construct another set of objects.

The U.S. Lesson

U.S. teachers at times also follow the pattern of instruction-practice-feedback (see figure 2). They simply do not do it as frequently as Japanese teachers. U.S. teachers would more likely begin the class period by explaining the formula for finding the

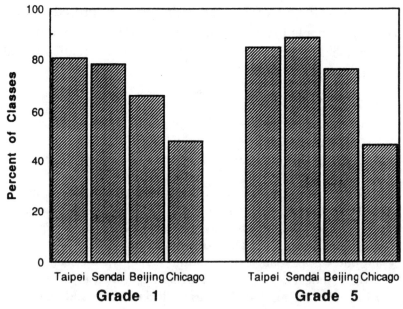

Figure 2.   Classes in Which Teacher Followed the Pattern of Instruction, Practice, and Feedback (in percent)

area of a right triangle. U.S. teachers would also more likely leave students to work on their own for longer periods. In our observations in U.S. classrooms, fifth-grade students spent more than 40 percent of their time doing such seat work. Because the seat work was likely to be assigned during the last half of the class period and time frequently ran out, there was no immediate feedback about the correctness of their solutions during more than half of the lessons.

Teachers' Lives

According to our interviews with teachers and teachers' responses to TIMSS questionnaires, the difference in teaching style between East Asian and U.S. teachers is due, in part, to the fact that U.S. teachers are required to be in front of their classes, teaching, for a much greater proportion of the time each week than are East Asian teachers. For example, according to the TIMSS data, eighth-grade mathematics teachers in the United States reported teaching twenty-six periods a week; Japanese teachers, only sixteen. In our studies, U.S. high school teachers reported spending twenty-one hours a week teaching, compared with thirteen hours reported by Japanese teachers. Teachers in other East Asian countries also have light teaching loads. For example, high school teachers in both Beijing and Taipei reported teaching an average of fifteen hours a week.

Teachers in the United States are not only required to teach more classes but also are assigned other duties more often than teachers in East Asia. As a result, U.S. teachers have little time to talk with one another, to share lesson plans, to observe one another teach, or to work with individual children—all opportunities that occur frequently in East Asian schools. Considering all the demands made on teachers' time, both during class periods and during the rest of the day, it is not surprising that U.S. teachers fare less well in the classroom than do their East Asian counterparts.

Teachers' Attitudes

Teachers in the United States not only differ from the East Asian teachers in their teaching and other obligations but also hold attitudes that are not conducive to producing high academic achievement in their students. When high school teachers were asked to rate how well they thought they were doing as teachers, they portrayed a positive picture (see figure 3). With such a high degree of self-satisfaction, they may be less motivated to improve than is the case with East Asian teachers, who are less likely to give themselves such high ratings.

The high self-approval of U.S. teachers may come from using criteria for judging what characterizes a good teacher different from those used by teachers in East Asia. We asked teachers in

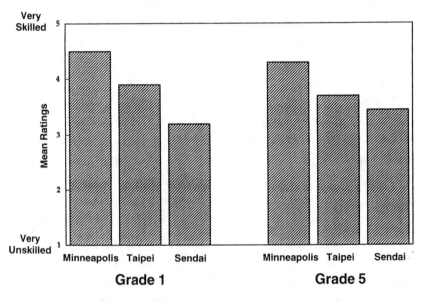

Figure 3.   Self-evaluation of Teachers concerning Their Teaching Skill in the United States, Taiwan, and Japan

Beijing and Chicago what characterizes a good teacher. Beijing teachers most frequently answered with the term *clarity;* Chicago teachers most frequently answered *sensitivity* (see figure 4). It seems reasonable to suggest that the effective transmission of information—one of the primary purposes of education—can be accomplished more readily by teachers who insist on clarity than by teachers who do not, regardless of how sensitive they may be. Teachers in both countries agreed that enthusiasm was also an important ingredient of good teaching.

Good Lessons

When we asked teachers about the elements of good teaching, we found a high degree of agreement. They said that in mathematics, for example, a good teacher makes the material meaningful, uses different examples, introduces concrete repre-

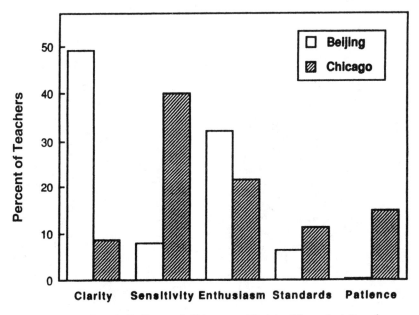

Figure 4. Teachers in Beijing and Chicago on Various Characteristics of a Good Teacher (in percent)

sentations of abstract concepts, discusses the relation of abstract rules to concrete problems, and involves students in solving problems and in evaluating alternative solutions.

When we asked teachers, both in Japan and in the United States, whether they agreed with these principles, all typically answered, "That's what we do!" The problem is that U.S. teachers are much less likely to carry out in their teaching what they agree are good teaching practices. A typical example indicates the percentage of lessons in the United States, Japan, Taiwan, and China in which the teacher made an explicit attempt to relate abstract rules to concrete problems (see figure 5).

Conclusion

Research in U.S. and East Asian classrooms strongly suggests that one of the underlying bases of the poor performance of U.S.

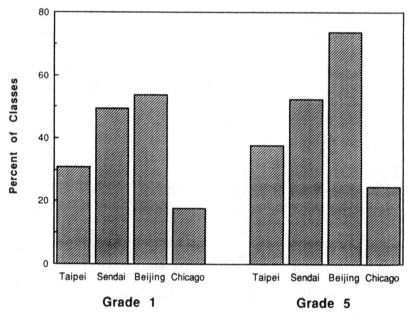

Figure 5.   Classes at Grades One and Five in Which Teacher Made an Explicit Effort to Relate Abstract Concepts to Concrete Examples (in percent)

students in comparative studies of students' achievement relates to differences in the educational systems and in the manner in which teaching is conducted. Teachers in the United States have neither the time nor the opportunity to work together to create the interesting, coherent, carefully planned lessons that are available to teachers in a country such as Japan. It seems unlikely, in fact, that rapid advancements will be made in the achievement of U.S. students until teachers are provided with the time necessary to master the content of the lessons they are teaching and to acquire the finely developed teaching techniques that ensure the most effective presentation of information.

Beliefs and Attitudes

Teachers' beliefs and practices are strongly influenced by the culture in which they live. If we find differences among teachers in the practices such as those just described, we would also expect to find large differences in the beliefs and attitudes of the parents and the students themselves. It is impossible to discuss all the attitudes and beliefs that we and others have found to be related to high academic achievement, but two of the major dimensions of difference will be described.

Motivation

One motivation for change is dissatisfaction with the status quo. If there is high agreement that conditions are satisfactory, there is little reason to consider changing current practices. This is as true in classrooms as it is in manufacturing plants. For example, U.S. companies, satisfied that they led the world in the production of automobiles, found themselves being crowded out of markets at the middle of the twentieth century by foreign companies. Not until they shed their high degree of self-satisfaction and became more attentive to improving the quality of their product were the U.S. companies able to regain the share of the market they had lost to their more enterprising foreign competitors.

A similar situation exists today in U.S. education. Despite the poor showing that U.S. students display in comparative studies, surveys reveal that U.S. parents in general express high degrees of satisfaction with their own children's academic accomplishments. For example, in studies involving several thousand mothers, we found that fewer than 10 percent of U.S. mothers of first- and fifth-graders we interviewed chose "not satisfied" when asked if they were "satisfied," "very satisfied," or "not satisfied" with their child's academic achievement. More than twice as many Chinese and Japanese mothers expressed dissatisfaction. Similarly, more than 40 percent of the U.S. mothers but fewer than 5 percent of the Chinese and Japanese mothers said they were "very satisfied." The same pattern of response was found when we asked fathers that question.

These attitudes may characterize parents in the two sets of cultures, but a critical question is whether the children share the same attitudes. Although U.S. parents may express high degrees of satisfaction with their children's academic achievement, their children may be more critical. To evaluate this possibility, we posed the same question to more than six thousand eleventh graders in North America (Minneapolis; Fairfax County, a suburb of Washington, D. C.; and Alberta, Canada) and East Asia (Taipei, Taiwan; Sendai, Japan; and Beijing, China).

The results how a marked difference between the responses of the students from North America and from East Asia (see figure 6). Fewer than a third of the North American students but more than three-fourths of the East Asian students said they were not satisfied with their academic performance. *Within* each of these two regions there is a remarkable similarity in the attitudes expressed by students.

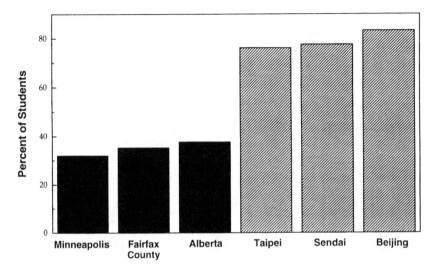

Figure 6.   Eleventh Graders Who Expressed Dissatisfaction with Their Current Academic Performance (in percent)

Why are North Americans so positive about their children's accomplishments? The most likely explanation is that they have low expectations for what their children can accomplish; low standards lead to a low percentage of parents who are dissatisfied with their children's performance. With so few dissatisfied parents, it is difficult to institute changes in the education system that will produce improvements in U.S. students' academic achievement.

Basis for Improvement

Not only do East Asian and Western parents differ in their degree of satisfaction with their children's performance, but they also differ in their beliefs about how that performance might be improved. For example, in East Asia the philosophy of Confucianism continues to be influential. According to this set of beliefs, human beings are malleable, subject to the environmental conditions under which they live. This view, initially applied to

moral behavior, has been gradually extended to all human behavior, and thus the avenue to success lies in the diligent application of effort. Nevertheless, innate differences among human
beings are recognized, for it is obvious that everyone does not
share the same physical or mental abilities. According to an old
Chinese saying, although a silk cloth remains silk when it is dyed
red, the important fact is that the color can be changed.

We attempted to evaluate the relative strength of their beliefs
in the possibility of changing their performance through effort
by presenting eleventh graders with the following situation:
"Here are some factors that may influence students' performance
in mathematics: A good teacher. Innate intelligence. Home environment. Studying hard. Which do you think is the most important factor?"

In line with Confucian precepts, more than half the Chinese
and Japanese students chose "Studying hard." Fewer than a
fourth of the North American students made this choice. In contrast, the majority of North American students chose "A good
teacher." The quality of the teacher was not a frequent choice
among the Chinese and Japanese students. In short, the East
Asian students assumed responsibility for their own progress,
whereas the North American students let others take responsibility for their performance.

Conclusion

It is easy to blame the problems in U.S. education on teachers
and teaching practices, but this would be an incomplete explanation. Although there is clearly a need for improvement in
teaching practices, this cannot occur without stronger support by
members of U.S. society. The problem is not primarily a financial

one. It is derived, in part, from two aspects of U.S. culture that do not lead to a recognition that such support is needed. First, students, as well as their parents, express satisfaction with their academic achievement, thereby reducing their motivation to seek improvement. A second belief that is equally unproductive for instituting change is for students to deny their own role in successful performance.

Producing the kinds of changes that might make the United States number one in the world, not by the year 2000 but possibly some time in the next century, will require the development of more-effective teaching practices, higher academic standards, and the acceptance of the belief that all students, through their own efforts, are capable of improvement. These are not easy changes to make, but they are necessary if we are to maintain our status in an increasingly competitive world.

References

Lee, S. Y., T. Graham, and H. W. Stevenson. 1996. "Teachers and Teaching: Elementary Schools in Japan and the United States." In T. Rohlen and G. LeTendre, eds., *Teaching and Learning in Japan*. New York: Cambridge University Press. Pp. 519–35.

McKnight, C. C., F. J. Crosswhite, J. A. Dossey, E. Kifer, N. O. Swafford, K. J. Travers, and T. J. Cooney. 1987. *The Underachieving Curriculum: Assessing U.S. School Mathematics from an International Perspective.* Champaign, Ill.: Stipes.

Peak, L. 1996. *Pursuing Excellence: A Study of U.S. Eighth-Grade Mathematics and Science Teaching, Learning, Curriculum, and Achievement in International Context.* Washington, D.C.: U.S. Government Printing Office.

———. 1997. *Pursuing Excellence: A Study of U.S. Fourth-Grade Mathematics and Science Teaching, Learning, Curriculum, and Achievement in International Context.* Washington, D.C.: U.S. Government Printing Office.

Stevenson, H. W., J. W. Stigler, G. W. Lucker, S. Y. Lee, C. C. Hsu, and

S. Kitamura. 1987. "Classroom Behavior and Achievement of Japanese, Chinese, and American Children." In R. Glaser, ed., *Advances in Instructional Psychology.* Hillsdale, N.J.: Erlbaum. Pp. 153–204.

Stigler, J. W. 1996. "The TIMSS Videotape Study." Manuscript. University of California at Los Angeles.

Maureen DiMarco

Measurement and Reform

Throughout the history of American public education, the call for change has been perhaps the one constant element, and it has constituted the clarion call of the education reformers. An analysis of the many attempts at change will yield a fairly consistent pattern of alternating among three different approaches to reform.

The first category of change is structural reform. This has been by far the most frequent of the reform categories, as it is the easiest to achieve. Structural reform is based on the notion that "if only we change how the system is organized, or looks, then all will improve in public education." Reforms in the structural category have included

- Centralization and decentralization
- Creating more layers of accountability or streamlining the layers
- Unification of small districts or breakup of large ones
- Requiring more reports or eliminating paperwork
- Electing trustees at large or electing trustees by area
- Parent or community councils

- Class-size reduction

The second most prevalent types of reforms have been process reforms based on the belief that "if only we changed the way education is delivered, all will improve in public schools." Reforms in the process category have included

- Individualized instruction
- Learning contracts
- Team teaching
- Cooperative learning
- Multiage grouping
- Open classrooms
- Learning centers

The third, and less easy to achieve but nonetheless recurrent reform, is content reform. Here the prevailing belief is "if only we change the curriculum, all will be well in the public schools." Reforms in the process category have included

- Removing all state requirements for graduation
- Legislating increased graduation requirements
- Old math, new math, new-new math
- Whole language, phonics, balanced literacy
- Setting standards
- Changing the type of testing

Yet while we have continually changed, or more accurately, rotated, structure, process, and content, we have also increasingly changed who makes the decisions about what to change.

Although there have always been pressures on local schools and districts from the political system, for the most part the decisions to adopt any one of these reforms were formerly made primarily at the local level.

Since the early 1970s, when the first educational funding equity lawsuit, *Serrano v. Priest*, was successfully brought in California, the court decisions attempting to equalize the disparities in per-pupil funding have increasingly placed the responsibility for funding education at the state level.

It is a political truism that those who must take the political heat for raising the money for public programs will always insist on having a significant say in how it is spent. Thus, more and more of the "reforms" in public education are driven from the top down by legislators who often have little or no education-related background beyond having attended school.

Today in virtually every state legislature and state department of education, the pressure is on to change something in the hope of improving student achievement. The word *hope* is most appropriate because the greatest frustration of lawmaking is that one cannot legislate outcome or product. One can only legislate structure, process, and content with an expectation that they may lead to the desired outcome.

A perfect example of how battles over curriculum and testing have reached high levels of political and public visibility can be found in California. In 1996, Governor Pete Wilson and the legislature poured more than $2 billion into repairing the reading and mathematics curricula, reducing class sizes and teacher training related to both. This alone dramatically increased the political pressure to be able to find out if the changes work (i.e., are the students learning?). And as everyone knows, the best way to do that is to give the children a test. Sounds simple. Yet as anyone who has been in California public education over the past ten years knows, it is not so simple.

In the 1970s and 1980s the California testing system was the California Assessment Program (CAP), a matrix sample, criterion-referenced test that did not yield individual results and did not allow schools or districts or the state to compare student achievement with that in the rest of the nation. By the late 1980s, increasing frustration with the assessment led to the beginnings of exploration of a new testing system. This process, however, was hastened by the veto of CAP by then Governor George Deukmejian in an act of pique over actions by then Superintendent of Public Instruction Bill Honig unrelated to testing. CAP was last administrated in 1989; the last results were reported in 1990.

Following the election of a new governor (Pete Wilson), Superintendent Honig, Senator Gary Hart, and I, on behalf of the governor, set out to create a new, and better, testing system. The result of our efforts came to be known as the California Learning Assessment System (CLAS).

CLAS was designed in legislation to achieve four fundamental goals. First, the test was to yield individual test scores so that every parent, teacher, and student had a clear view of that individual student's strengths and weaknesses. Second, the test was to be balanced between multiple choice and open-ended performance items, thus measuring both basic skills and application skills. Third, the test was to create a world-class scale that allowed testing comparisons with the rest of the country and, eventually, other nations. Fourth, the test was to be developed using the expertise of the professional testing industry.

Forty million dollars later, we had a test that gave no individual scores, tested no basic skills, was related to a scale no one could explain, and never used the expertise of professional measurement experts. Perversely, the controversies that erupted over CLAS were first focused on the test's content and political correctness or lack thereof. Huge debates raged over the appropriateness of selections, and charges were leveled of intrusiveness. Yet the larger problems with CLAS were in the academic content and technical deficiencies. Although much has been written about the ill-fated CLAS test, the single largest reason for its demise was the California Department of Education's insisting that no one could see the test to ascertain if the charges were true. Testing security is an important issue to be sure, but forbidding state legislators from privately viewing the test under secure circumstances was undoubtedly the final fatal act for the test.

The real issues underlying the problems with CLAS were not apparent until well after its formal veto and defunding. As forms of the test were finally revealed, it became apparent that many of the problems were related to the California Department of Education's promoting a methodology of instruction that the public did not understand; nor did it reflect the public's views. This was best reflected in the mathematics sections, where scoring rewarded students for writing essays explaining work and answers that were wrong but penalized students for the correct answers if the written essay was deficient. This led to a belated look at the mathematics textbook adoption about to be completed by the State Board of Education.

On reviewing the draft Curriculum Commission evaluation of textbooks submitted for approval for use in California, even more disturbing changes were found than those in the CLAS test. The opening overview said, "Early memorization of number facts is seen as a hindrance rather than a help in mastering mathematics concepts." Reviews rewarded textbooks that emphasized discovery over computation. Teachers were encouraged to "coach" instead of instruct. Textbooks with practice problems were penalized as "drill to kill." A sample letter to send parents admonished parents "to not impose your own mathematical values on your child. Children are very creative and will invent their own ways of doing math." This led to my infamous "fuzzy crap" quote in Debra Saunders's syndicated column in the *San Francisco Chronicle.*

As the governor's representative, I thought it was imperative to try to stop such nonsense and insist on adopting textbooks that contained basic mathematical computation as well as mathematics concepts. Yet this was not easily achieved. The State Board, after much debate and testimony from department staff claiming that "children will not need basic skills in the twenty-first century," added three textbook series to the list for adoption over the strenuous objections of the Department of Education.

Meanwhile, back on the testing front, the legislature was readying another piece of legislation to create a testing system that would measure student achievement. This time the bill (AB 265) was designed with the expectation that the language of the bill would allow the selection of three to five nationally norm-referenced tests that would allow comparability among tests and with other states and the nation, while still maintaining some local choice. Unfortunately, the State Department of Education again decided to redefine the law and discarded the comparability requirement, ultimately approving more than fifty tests for local district use and thus rendering state and national comparisons impossible.

Two years after the passage of AB 265 and after the multibillion dollar investment in reading and math and class-size reduction, political forces led by Governor Wilson asked how the students were doing. The response—that it was not possible to tell with more than fifty tests in use—caused the governor to insist on a single, off-the-shelf, nationally norm-referenced test for all students in grades 2 through 11.

Although California has now gone nearly a decade without any systematic statewide measurement of student achievement, results on the National Assessment of Educational Progress

(NAEP) have hastened the ugency of both the testing and the curricular reforms. In reading, both in 1992 and again in 1994, the NAEP showed California fourth-grade students scoring near the bottom when compared with fourth graders in all participating states.

The resultant retreat from whole language and constructivist math to a more phonics-based reading curriculum and skills-based mathematics curriculum, and the call for a new testing system, clearly reflected the frustration of not being able to legislate product or results. This trend is not unique to California by any means. The last twelve months of news articles related to testing reveal a stunning trend:

- Battles over testing in Maryland, Virginia, Colorado, Illinois, New York, Vermont, Minnesota
- Parents suing over the use of test results in North Carolina
- Parents refusing to allow their children to take the Michigan state test

And then there is Kentucky, where every horror story possible seems to have happened with the KIRIS test. KIRIS was supposed to be an incentivized, high-stakes, open-ended, performance-based, criterion-referenced test linked to NAEP that yielded individual and group longitudinal, norm-referenced-like results for instruction, diagnosis, prescription, curriculum improvement, and teacher evaluation. Piece of cake. (This is what we in the testing world call Vegematic Testing. It must do all things for all people and clean the kitchen when it's over. Yet how appealing it is to those who have no real understanding of what scientific measurement is about.) In Kentucky, front-page articles appeared daily about cheating, schools that drastically changed their curricula in response to low scores only to find out that the scores were wrong, districts suing the state over changes in scoring, and the attorney general of Kentucky ruling that the tests were "arbitrary and unfair." The collapse of KIRIS has put many of the reforms in Kentucky at risk in the public and political eyes. The inability to prove that the test accurately measures student achievement has had devastating effects on every school district in Kentucky. Failing to understand the key issues of reliability, validity, feasibility, comparability, and fairness damaged more than the test. It damaged the schools' credibility.

For those who grapple with the need to measure student achievement, particularly to determine the success or lack of it related to reforms of all types, it is critical that we recognize the different audiences for testing and their desires for various types of information. Parents' most basic question is, "How is my child doing?" They wish to know what skills their children have learned, which they have not, and how they compare with the other students in the class, the school, the district, and the state and nation. And they particularly want to know what to do to help their children succeed. For teachers, the question evolves to "How am I teaching?" They need to know how the class is progressing, which areas of learning need to be emphasized, and have they covered all the material to be taught. The school administrator wants to know "How do I improve the school?" She needs group data so she can compare classrooms and determine how best to allocate time and resources to improve learning. The district superintendent and school board want tests that tell the community and voters how their district is doing. They also need to use data to allocate personnel and resources to improve learning and to ensure accountability to the taxpayers who pay for the schools and vote in the next election. State officials (and now the federal government) want tests to answer the question "How successful are our schools and children?" as demanded by their constituents and taxpayers. They also will make decisions related to resources and political agendas based on the tests' information.

These agendas and needs do not all point to one kind of test. When comparisons of students, schools, districts, and states based on national standards are desired, a nationally normed test is the only instrument that can answer the question. When the questions relate to instructional methods or unique state or local curricular standards, a criterion-referenced test is the best choice. When measurement of the system is the goal, matrix sampling is effective, but if individual scores are needed, matrix sampling will not meet the need.

The clear lessons of the testing battles are that we must be clear about what we are measuring. We must know what the test results mean and do not mean. And, perhaps most important, we must understand the devastating impacts that can result if we do not use solid, research-based measurement. Measuring teaching and measuring learning are both legitimate purposes of testing but should not be confused. One is a measurement of process, and the other is measurement of outcome or product. The "system" wants to measure process, but the parents, public, and politicians want to measure results.

Getting people outside the measurement community to understand what a test means and does not mean is probably the most frustrating task of all. The temptations to use data are almost too seductive to overcome. We Americans have a love-hate relationship with data. We use them if we agree with them, and we disparage them if we do not. Mark Twain's old quip "There are three kinds of lies; lies, damned lies and statistics" is still the prevailing notion among those disagreeing with data disproving their position. We use data to spring into action but usually ignore their real implications.

One superintendent recently stated, "We have been using the Iowa Tests for fifteen years and lately the scores have gone down. Clearly we need a new test." The data got his attention, but he didn't consider the variable to be the fact that his district had implemented whole language and constructivist math. Instead he wanted a test that supported his instructional bias.

Many years ago, as an earlier debate over testing raged, Harry Handler, former superintendent of the Los Angeles Unified School District and a professor of statistics at the UCLA Graduate School of Education, made an observation that is worth remembering. Handler commented that all these new testing ideas were intriguing, interesting, and certainly worth considering. There was this one little thing nagging at the back of his mind, however: "How come the only time we want to change the test is when the students aren't doing well?" If one looks at the list of states performing at the bottom of the NAEP rankings, one finds an almost perfect match with those states instituting new reading programs and new tests. Perhaps those are the states that should do both of those things. Without knowing what educational measurement is about and what types of tests are most appropriate for the purposes intended, however, these states could easily find themselves yet again looking for another test or another reading program without really knowing what it is that their students need.

E. D. Hirsch Jr.

Research-Based Education Policy

The enormous problem in basing policy on research is that it is almost impossible to make educational policy that is *not* based on research. Almost every educational practice that has ever been pursued has been supported with data by somebody. I don't know a single failed policy, ranging from the naturalistic teaching of reading to the open classroom to the teaching of abstract set-theory in third-grade math, that hasn't been research based. Experts have advocated almost every conceivable practice short of inflicting permanent bodily harm.

So we need to discriminate between reliable and unreliable research. And of course my recommendation is going to be that only reliable research should guide policy. Now it is possible to give some rules of thumb for determining scientific reliability, but there is no formula adequate to all situations. The distinguished sociologist of science Stephen Cole, in his book *Making Science*,[1] has found a continuous spectrum of reliability in most of the natural and social sciences. At the core of each discipline, there develops a consensus of the learned, and this consensus is

This is a revised and edited version of an address to the California State Board of Education, April 10, 1997.
   1. Stephen Cole, *Making Science* (Cambridge, Mass.: Harvard University Press, 1992).

highly dependable. It is close enough to being right that you can bet your life and your children's lives on that core. But out at the edge, on the frontier of the discipline, there is considerable disagreement, and we can't tell for sure which rival theory is right. When lawmakers say that educational policy should be based on research, the spirit of the law implies reliable consensus research. Any other interpretation would mean, and has meant, carrying out unwarranted human experimentation on our children.

If this distinction between core and noncore research is rightly understood, and if its implications are followed in California, then I think the days of faddism, guruism, partisanship, and unwarranted experimentation may be numbered. I'm not saying that research can decide the *aims* of education. In a democracy, those are decided by the people. But core science *can* determine how best to achieve them. Take reading. As a people we have decided that we want all our children to read well. Mainstream research has been saying for some years that a naturalistic approach cannot achieve that goal for all children. The reason that core research was not heeded is a subject for intellectual and social history, some of which I traced in my recent book, *The Schools We Need and Why We Don't Have Them*.[2]

I was forced to conclude that, in the field of psychology, which is the key field for education research, much of what is accepted within the educational community has been required to conform to a so-called constructivist ideology that does *not* represent the consensus in mainstream psychology and is almost certainly incorrect. One distinguished psychologist, who receives grants from the education division of the National Science Foundation (NSF), expressed dismay at the ideological, antiem-

---

2. E. D. Hirsch Jr., *The Schools We Need and Why We Don't Have Them* (New York: Doubleday, 1996).

pirical sermons, as he called them, which he hears at the education division of the NSF.

Insisting on ideological conformity makes for unreliable science. It hinders the best research from getting disseminated to the education world—to journalists, policymakers, publishers, teachers, and administrators. As a result, there is an information gap regarding the findings of mainstream psychology as applied to education.

This situation is reminiscent of what happened to biology in the Soviet Union under Lysenkoism, a theory that bears similarities to constructivism. In Stalin's day, Lysenko was the powerful bureaucrat-scientist who controlled Soviet biological research and declined to fund any that didn't conform to the received ideology, which consisted in the view that nurture can transform nature. During the Lysenko period, the dominance of this ideology over disinterested research retarded Soviet biology and caused mass starvation. There are analogies lurking in that history. Over the door of every board of education should be posted the watchwords Remember Lysenko.

Let me illustrate with one recent incident. The premier journal of educational research is *Educational Researcher*. Recently, an article was submitted that refuted the claims of situated learning.[3] (Situated learning is the supposed scientific basis of such teaching methods as project learning, integrated learning, and thematic learning). The article also refuted the claims of constructivism, which is a supposedly scientific foundation for such teaching methods as inquiry learning, discovery learning, and hands-on learning. After a so-called peer review, *Educational Researcher* turned down the article and agreed to print only a sec-

3. "Applications and Misapplications of Cognitive Psychology to Mathematics Education," http://sands.psy.cmsu.edu/ACT/papers/misapplied-abs-ja.html.

tion of its critique of situated learning. This decision would have been unremarkable except that the three authors of the article happened to be among the most distinguished cognitive scientists in the world, John Anderson and two other colleagues at Carnegie-Mellon, Lynn Reder and Herb Simon. The latter happens also to be a Nobel Prize winner.

No knowledgeable and disinterested person should doubt that Anderson, Reder, and Simon are far more likely than their journal reviewers to be expressing the consensus view at the core of mainstream psychology. It is safe to bet that they are much more likely to be right than the peer reviewers chosen by *Educational Researcher*. This is a clear example of how educational Lysenkoism closes off important and sometimes critical sources of scientific information.

Research can't flourish under such intellectual conformity. It's our collective duty to make sure that journalists, educators, and policymakers have access to the best information from mainstream science. If scientific information had been allowed to flow more freely during the past two decades, the school scene would have a different face than it does now. California math and reading scores would almost certainly be higher.

Over the past decades, educational Lysenkoism has created a conflict between the conclusions promulgated widely in education and those that are accepted in mainstream psychology. Of several such conflicts I shall choose three of the most important—testing, math, and early education. I intend to be blunt, since forthrightness will be more useful to you than tact. I won't revisit reading research, since California has made policy that is consistent with what is agreed on by such top researchers as Adams, Foorman, and Stanovich.[4]

In each of the three cases, I shall briefly outline the conflicts

4. Marilyn Jager Adams, Barbara Foorman, Keith Stanovich.

between educational Lysenkoism and mainstream science, and then I'll list the names of a few highly regarded scientists whom you could consult with confidence. To make my comments as useful as possible, I will make some informed predictions about what those top researchers would tell you. I got the names by asking a number of highly reputed scientists which colleagues they considered to be the most authoritative persons in their field, and I found there was wide agreement about those names. As Cole points out, we need to depend ultimately on the consensus views of scientists who are regarded as tops in their fields by other scientists. Should doubt arise as to who those persons are, one should ask for guidance from the National Academy of Sciences. It does not make sense to depend any longer on the guru principle.

It is a paradox that I should be offering advice about assessment here in California, where you have the recognized dean of the subject, Professor Lee Cronbach of Stanford. As you know, there is a rage in education circles for so-called performance assessments. I'd like to know what Professor Cronbach would say about the widespread rush to use these expensive and undependable modes of testing. Despite the tendency of a large body of psychometric research, the current position of the educational community is that performance tests are superior to multiple-choice tests. Educators and state legislatures have hastened to mandate these hugely expensive and unreliable instruments as high-stakes, summative assessments. Recently, the *Wall Street Journal* printed a front-page article about the confusing consequences of performance testing in Michigan.[5] Before California joins the crowd, I would advise you to consult Professor Cron-

5. June Krunholz, "If You Have Brains, You Might Decide to Skip This Test," *Wall Street Journal*, March 28, 1997. See also E. D. Hirsch Jr., letter to the editor, April 26, 1997.

bach, if you haven't already, or other top researchers such as Samuel Messick. The answers you get from them will be reliable ones.

They are likely to tell you that performance assessments are good for classroom use. And they would probably concede that a writing sample should be a component of any writing test, if only to make sure that the right message about doing a large amount of writing in school is sent out to students and teachers. But core research says that performance assessments are the least reliable and the most expensive tests that exist. Top scientists in the field would advise you against using end-of-year performance tests if your aim is to use assessments that are accurate, dependable, and reasonably priced. Specialists will also tell you that almost all the nasty things said about multiple-choice tests are incorrect.

This example illustrates an important principle about reliability. Scientific consensus is not just a matter of counting heads. If you counted all the experts who have gotten on board the performance test bandwagon, they would outnumber by far the toilers in the psychometric vineyards who publish meticulous articles in the best journals. Counting heads is not the way to determine a scientific consensus. The number of people who believe in flying saucers is greater than than the number of astrophysicists in the world.

I am making the perhaps disagreeable point that science is an elitist subject and ought to be so. The consensus that counts is the consensus of the learned. That kind of consensus is determined by disinterested, high-quality peer review in high-quality journals. In cases of disagreement, that's why you should stick to people like Professor Cronbach. In the end, of course, only evidence and argument count in science. But there is evidence and evidence, argument and argument. It is an uncomfortable thing to say, but the average quality and reliability of science in the best educational journals is below the quality and reliability of science in the best mainstream psychology journals. We laypersons cannot judge the quality of research. Figures don't lie, but how do we know which figures are accurate, complete, and rightly interpreted? Our only recourse is to depend on the reputations of the most highly regarded journals and scientists. Sensible persons would not quickly challenge Lee Cronbach any more than they would challenge a Nobelist like Herb Simon. Such highly regarded sources are not always right, but they are far more *likely* to be right. The consensus of the learned in first-rate scientific work is one of the closest connections we have with the reality principle.

Let me turn to math education. I read a recent report in *Education Week* that stated that there were two rival math groups in California vying for your approval. On the one side there is what *Education Week* called the *reform* group, who want to put in place the standards of the National Council of Teachers of Mathematics (NCTM) and on the other the so-called antireform group that calls those standards variously *fuzzy math* and *whole math.* I thought that the tone of the *Education Week* report was typical of current educational reporting in that the NCTM approach, which reflects the dominant view among educators, was labeled *reform,* whereas the dissident group that is trying to effect change was labeled *antireform.* That kind of ideological bias in reporting is characteristic of the education world, and it well illustrates the need for constant vigilance.

I hardly need to restate the details of the math debate. The NCTM group stresses conceptual understanding over mindless drill and practice, whereas the dissident group stresses the need for drill and practice leading to mastery. To resolve the issue, which researchers should you listen to? Here are three suggestions: John Anderson, David Geary, and Robert Siegler, three highly distinguished scientists in the psychology of math education. What are they likely to tell you? I believe you will get strong agreement from them on the following points: that varied and repeated practice leading to rapid recall and automaticity is necessary to higher-order problem-solving skills in both mathematics and the sciences.

They would probably explain to you that lack of automaticity places limits on the mind's channel capacity for higher-order problem-solving skills. They would tell you that only intelligently directed and repeated practice, leading to fast, automatic recall of math facts, and facility in computation and algebraic manipulation can lead one to effective real-world problem solving. Anderson, Geary, and Siegler would provide you with reliable facts, figures, and documentation to support their position, and these data would come not just from isolated lab experiments but also from large-scale classroom results. If these top scientists agreed on all these points, that is the consensus you should trust, no matter how many pronouncements to the contrary might be made by national educational bodies.

Speaking of national educational bodies brings me to my third and last example of conflict between educational research and mainstream research. To my mind, it is the most fateful conflict of all since it touches on the general quality of our educational system and its ability to realize the dream of the common school, that is, the dream of providing genuine equality of educational opportunity to all students regardless of their backgrounds. There is a national body called the National Association for the Education of Young Children, NAEYC. It withholds its approval from schools and preschools that fail to follow what it calls *developmentally appropriate practice*. In its policy statements, it considers it developmentally inappropriate for a whole class to listen to a teacher as a group or for children to learn academic topics that are deemed too abstract, too challenging, too advanced, or too . . . inappropriate. I have heard NAEYC experts state that the Eiffel Tower is developmentally inappropriate and also James Monroe, though not James Madison.

Who are top researchers to whom you might turn to ask whether this position is sound? What does consensus mainstream science say about the appropriateness of giving young children challenging academic instruction in preschool through third grade? Two top scientists from California would be Rochel Gelman at the University of California at Los Angeles or, looking east, Kevin Miller at the University of Illinois. Or, looking west, Sandra Scarr would fly in from Hawaii to advise you if you beckoned. There are many other names. Any scientist who has kept up with this field would tell you that there is no foundation in fact or in desirable practice for withholding challenging content from young children.

In my recent book I discussed this discrepancy between the Romantic doctrines of the NAEYC and the findings of mainstream research. Since the book appeared, the Carnegie Foundation has issued a report called "Years of Promise," which also shows that the dominant ideas about developmental appropriateness are not science but ideology. The overwhelming evidence against the positions of the NAEYC recently caused that body subtly to revise its guidelines. But the revision is skin-deep and doesn't openly admit that a retreat has occurred, and even that slight shift has not filtered down to experts in early childhood education, who still pronounce on *developmentally appropriate practice.*

What advice would the scientists give? They would certainly reject many of the still-current positions of the NAEYC that still powerfully dominate the education world. These researchers would encourage you to create challenging, content-rich academic programs for all young children. They would say that programs like Head Start—if fortified with coherent goals and academically rich content, and if followed by coherent goals and academically rich content in kindergarten and first and second grades—would enable students to overcome many of our current educational defects and inequities.

I have saved this supremely important topic for my final example of the pervasive conflict between science and educational ideology. The doctrine of developmentally appropriate practice is drummed into almost all teachers who take early education courses. The intention is to ensure caring treatment for young children, yet the ultimate effect of the doctrine is to cause social harm. To withhold demanding content from young children between preschool and third grade has an effect that is quite different from the one intended. It leaves advantaged children (who get knowledge at home) with boring pablum, and it condemns disadvantaged children to a permanent educational handicap that grows worse over time. We know that early education can overcome many of these deficits, and we also know that what is called *developmentally appropriate practice* cannot.

This doctrine and the practices that stem from it are largely responsible for the educational inadequacies that led to the recent controversy over Ebonics. It wasn't a difference between black and white English that ultimately created desperation in Oakland. It was a much more general educational failure. Much-needed content and language skills are not being taught to all our children at an early age. William Julius Wilson makes this point in his recent book on the urban ghetto, *When Work Disappears*. Disadvantaged children need precisely the sort of learning that is falsely called developmentally inappropriate. Nor are just black children being penalized by withholding the early knowledge needed for educational success. The withholding of an academic and verbal focus in early education generally handicaps *all* children, especially disadvantaged ones. As the late, great James Coleman showed, it is ineffective early schooling coupled with economic class, not with race or ethnicity, that causes the academic achievement gap.

I think you would get consensus from mainstream science on the following prediction: that if we bring all children to readiness in the early grades, then the achievement of excellence and equity in later grades will begin to be possible. I would to begin to shift large resources into academically effective early education. In due course, such a policy would loosen up a lot of remedial money that could be spent on improving early education still more. Overcoming the inadequacies of early education is the most effective way of preventing the inadequacies that exist at twelfth grade.

Yet the phrase *developmentally appropriate practice* has been effective politically. It has played on our love and solicitude for young children. It is used as a kind of conversation stopper. If one is told that an educational recommendation is *developmentally inappropriate*, one is supposed to retreat and remove the offending item from the early curriculum. But this retreat has to stop. We must stand up to unsupported rhetorical bullying and rely on the people who know the research. To cave in to intimidating rhetoric is to harm our children, not help them. The Romantic doctrine of NAEYC is wasting minds and perpetuating social inequities.

Let me close with some graphs from the winter 1996–1997 issue of *American Educator*, put out by the American Federation of Teachers (AFT), Al Shanker's union. First, the cover illustrates developmentally inappropriate practice at work, with an enthusiastic first grader saying,

My name is Jose Castro-Rodriguez. I'm in the first grade, and right now we're learning about Ancient Egypt—about the sarcophagus—that's what they put the mummies in: and how they got the bodies ready to be mummies and which body parts they put into the canopic jars—they threw away the brain because they thought the heart did the thinking; and how they had to make sure no one finds out where the mummies were, because you're not supposed to mess with dead people; and how they used an ostrich feather to measure the heart, and if it was little that meant you had been good and could go to the next life; and about the different kinds of canopic jars and about the different Egyptian gods. And we've been learning about King Tut . . .

I also know a lot about the Aztecs. Do you want me to tell you about that, too?

Now, here's a page with some graphs (see figures 1 and 2). The editor, Liz McPike of the AFT, tried to show graphically some of the educational benefits of being developmentally *inap*-propriate. I'm not using these graphs, by the way, to recommend the core knowledge sequence since you probably know that I am prejudiced in its favor. I'm simply recommending that you de-mand an early curriculum that is equally rich and effective and equally inappropriate. One of the greatest services we can pro-vide to our children would be to start inducing self-doubt in

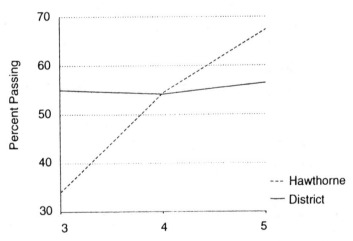

Figure 1.   Texas Assessment of Academic Skills Reading Performance, San Antonio, Texas, 1994

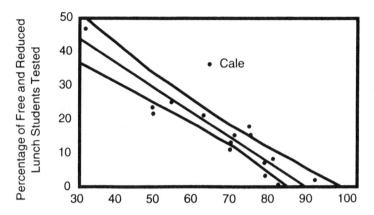

Percentage of Students Testing Above the 50th National Percentile
Diagonal bands show predicted performance range

Figure 2. Iowa Test of Basic Skills Score Performance in Relation to Free/
Reduced-Price Lunch, Albemarle County, Virginia, 1996

those early childhood experts who have been wielding the word *inappropriate* like a battle-ax.

Figure 1 shows the progress made by disadvantaged children who start off below the district norm but who, after a couple of years of having a rich, coherent, and inappropriate curriculum, catch up with and exceed their advantaged peers who are following the typically fragmented, incoherent, and *appropriate* sort.

Figure 2 indicates the same sort of equity and excellence effects in a different way. On the vertical are the percentage of students who are on free and reduced lunches. On the horizontal are the percentage of students who score above average. Each dot represents the performance of a school. This district has just one developmentally inappropriate school. You can guess which one it is. In the other schools, academic achievement is inexorably and precisely linked to social class. Both of these graphs illustrate that a rich and coherent early curriculum improves performance for all but improves it most for disadvantaged students, thus narrowing the equity gap—just as Coleman predicted in his massive study *Equality of Educational Opportunity*. In short, if you want to achieve excellence and equity, you have to withstand the accusation of being developmentally inappropriate.

But, true to my theme, let me close by cautioning you to look with just as cold an eye on *my* data as you would those of any other educational guru. What do reliable experts say about these assertions? Is this a practice that has proved itself on a large scale? What is the consensus of top-notch researchers in the field?

Those should be the constant questions asked in research-based policy. I hope I have helped clarify what the term *research based* ought to mean in practice. I earnestly hope you will follow this great principle.

Appendix

Conference Agenda

HOOVER INSTITUTION SYMPOSIUM
What's Gone Wrong in America's Classrooms?

Stauffer Auditorium
Herbert Hoover Memorial Building
Stanford University
February 24–25, 1997

Agenda

Monday, February 24

1:00 P.M. **Welcome**
John Raisian, Director, Hoover Institution
Introduction
Williamson Evers, Hoover Institution

1:10 P.M. **Fundamental Issues**
Williamson Evers, "From Progressive Education to Discovery Learning"
John R. Anderson, Carnegie-Mellon University; "Cognitive Psychology and Instruction"
Bonnie Grossen, University of Oregon; "Research-Based Educational Reform"

3:15 P.M. **Core Subjects**
Jack M. Fletcher, University of Texas-Houston Medical School; "Reading: A Scientific Approach"
Louisa Cook Moats, Dartmouth Medical School; "Language Structure and Teaching Spelling"
Harold Stevenson, University of Michigan; "Teaching Math"

6:30 P.M. STANFORD FACULTY CLUB
Speaker: Jaime Escalante, Hiram Johnson High School, Sacramento, California; "Stand and Deliver"

Tuesday, February 25

9:00 A.M. **State-Level Case Study**
Bill Honig, San Francisco State University; "What Went Wrong in California and How to Fix It"

10:15 A.M. **Classroom Practices, Accountability, and Efficacy in School Reform**
Maureen DiMarco, Riverside Publishing; "Testing"
Connie Jones, Core Knowledge Foundation; "Content-Based Curriculum"
Doug Carnine, University of Oregon; "Efficacy in Education Reform"

Contributors

MAUREEN DIMARCO, former secretary of the Office of Child Development and Education for the State of California, is now vice president of Riverside Publishing, which publishes the Iowa Tests of Basic Skills and the Stanford-Binet intelligence test. She was president of the California School Boards Association in 1990.

WILLIAMSON M. EVERS is a research fellow at the Hoover Institution at Stanford University, an adjunct associate professor of political science at Santa Clara University, and a commissioner of the California State Commission for the Establishment of Academic Content and Performance Standards. He is a member of the board of directors of the East Palo Alto Charter School and the editor of *National Service: Pro & Con* (1990).

JACK M. FLETCHER is a neuropsychologist whose research ranges from the neurobiology of reading disabilities to classroom reading interventions for disadvantaged children. He is a professor in the Department of Pediatrics and at the Center for Academic and Reading Skills at the University of Texas-Houston Medical School.

BONNIE GROSSEN is a research associate at the National Center to Improve the Tools of Educators at the University of Oregon. She is also the editor of *Effective School Practices*, the quarterly journal of the Association for Direct Instruction.

E. D. HIRSCH JR. is the president of the Core Knowledge Foundation and a professor of education and humanities at the University of Virginia. He is the author of *The Schools We Need and Why We Don't Have Them* (1996) and *Cultural Literacy* (1987).

BILL HONIG is a visiting professor at the School of Education at San Francisco State University and codirector of the Consortium on Reading Excellence. He was the California state superintendent of public instruction from 1983 to 1993 and is the author of *Teaching Our Children to Read* (1992) and *Last Chance for Our Children* (1985).

G. REID LYON is the chief of the Child Development and Behavior Branch of the National Institute of Child Health and Human Development at the National Institutes of Health.

LOUISA COOK MOATS is the project director of the Early Interventions Project in the District of Columbia Public Schools and a clinical associate professor in the Department of Pediatrics and at the Center for Academic and Reading Skills at the University of Texas-Houston Medical School. In 1996–97 she was a Distinguished Visiting Scholar at the Center for Improvement of Reading Instruction, Institute for Education Reform, California State University at Sacramento. She is the author of *Spelling: Development, Disability and Instruction* (1995).

HAROLD W. STEVENSON is a professor of psychology at the University of Michigan. He directed the ethnographic case studies project of the Third International Mathematics and Science Study (TIMSS) and is a past president of the Society for Research in

Child Development. During the past seventeen years his research has concentrated on investigating the beliefs, attitudes, and practices that underlie cross-national differences in academic achievement, primarily those related to East Asia and the United States. An overview of this work appears in *The Learning Gap* (1992), a book written with James Stigler.

Index